The Chester Book of Nursery Rhymes & Children's Songs

Chester Music
part of The Music Sales Group
London / New York / Paris / Sydney / Copenhagen / Berlin / Madrid / Tokyo

Alice The Camel

Traditional

Verse 2:
Alice the camel has four humps.
Alice the camel has four humps.
Alice the camel has four humps
So go, Alice, go.
Boom, boom, boom.

Verse 3:
Alice the camel has three humps.
Alice the camel has three humps.
Alice the camel has three humps
So go, Alice, go.
Boom, boom, boom.

Verse 4:
Alice the camel has two humps. *etc.*

Verse 5:
Alice the camel has one hump. *etc.*

Verse 6:
Alice the camel has no humps.
Alice the camel has no humps.
Alice the camel has no humps
So Alice is a horse!

All The Pretty Little Horses

Traditional

Lullaby

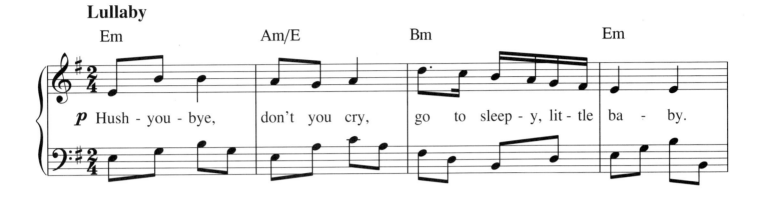

Hush - you - bye, don't you cry, go to sleep - y, lit - tle ba - by.

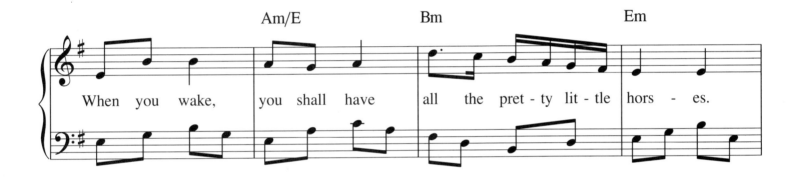

When you wake, you shall have all the pret - ty lit - tle hors - es.

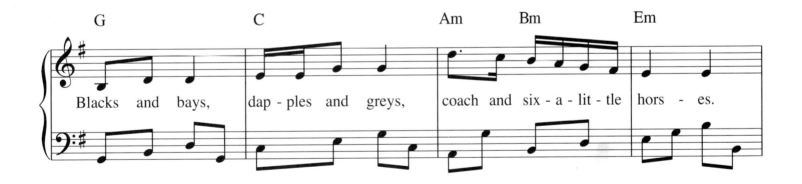

Blacks and bays, dap - ples and greys, coach and six - a - lit - tle hors - es.

Hush - you - bye, don't you cry, go to sleep - y, lit - tle ba - by.

Alouette, Gentille Alouette

Traditional

Alouette, gentille alouette;
Alouette, je te plumerai.
Je te plumerai la têt'*, Je te plumerai la têt'.
Et la têt', et la têt',
Alouett', Alouett',
Oh!

*Each time the chorus is sung, a part of the body is added, for example
le bec (beak); le nez (nose); les yeux (eyes); le cou (neck) *etc.*

The words mean: Little lark, I'm going to pluck your feathers.
I'll pluck your head (la têt')

A Tisket, A Tasket

Traditional

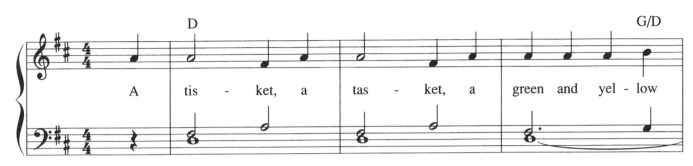

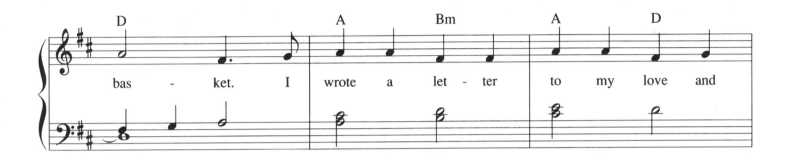

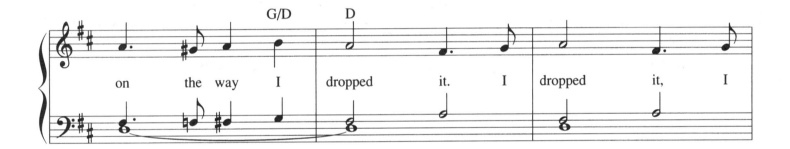

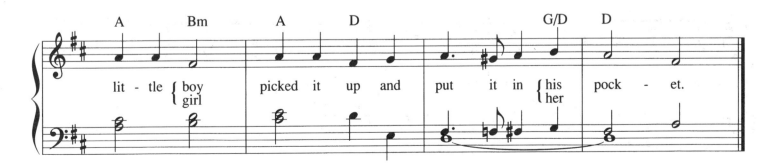

Animal Fair

Traditional

Brightly, in two (♩. = one beat)

went to the an - i - mal fair,_____ the birds and the beasts were

there._____ The big ba - boon by the light of the moon was

comb - ing his au - burn hair._____ The mon - key fell out of his

bunk, (clap) and slid down the el - e - phant's trunk, (wheee!) The

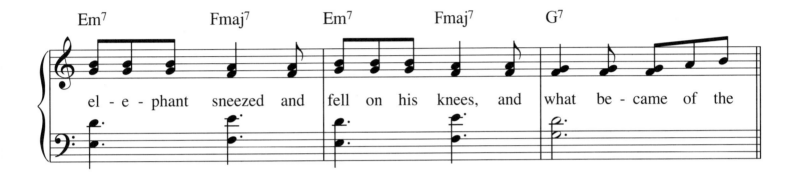

el - e - phant sneezed and fell on his knees, and what be - came of the

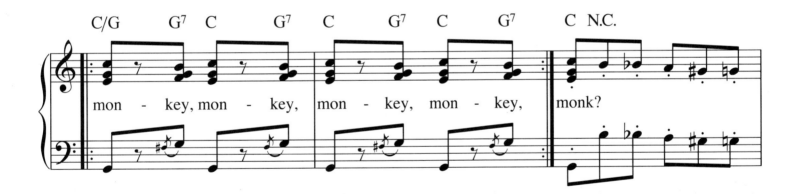

mon - key, mon - key, mon - key, mon - key, monk?

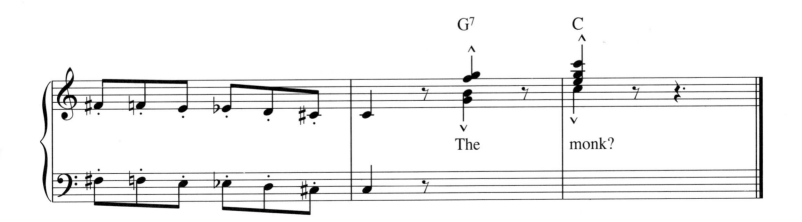

The monk?

A-Hunting We Will Go

Traditional

Jolly ♩ = 104

A - hunt-ing we will go, a - hunt-ing we will go, we'll

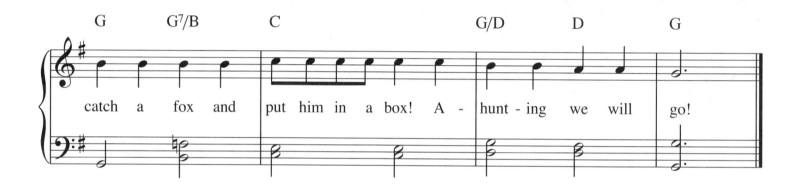

catch a fox and put him in a box! A - hunt-ing we will go!

Baby Bumble Bee

Traditional

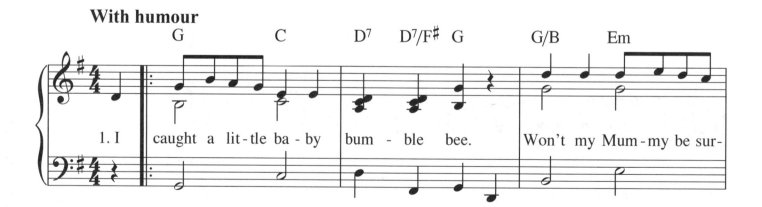

With humour

1. I caught a lit-tle ba-by bum - ble bee. Won't my Mum-my be sur-

- prised at me? I caught a lit-tle ba-by bum-ble bee.

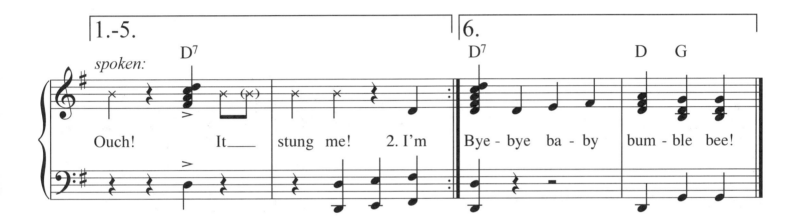

1.-5. *spoken:* Ouch! It____ stung me! 2. I'm

6. Bye - bye ba - by bum - ble bee!

Verse 2:
I'm squishin' up my baby bumble bee.
Won't my Mummy be surprised at me?
I'm squishin' up my baby bumble bee.
Yuk! What a mess!

Verse 3:
I'm lickin' up my baby bumble bee.
Won't my Mummy be surprised at me?
I'm lickin' up my baby bumble bee.
Ick! I feel sick!

Verse 4:
I'm barfin' up my baby bumble bee.
Won't my Mummy be surprised at me?
I'm barfin' up my baby bumble bee.
Oh! What a mess!

Verse 5:
I'm wipin' up my baby bumble bee.
Won't my Mummy be surprised at me?
I'm wipin' up my baby bumble bee.
Oops! Mummy's new towel!

Verse 6:
I'm wringin' out my baby bumble bee.
Won't my Mummy be surprised at me?
I'm wringing out my baby bumble bee.
Bye-Bye baby bumble bee!

Baa Baa Black Sheep

Traditional

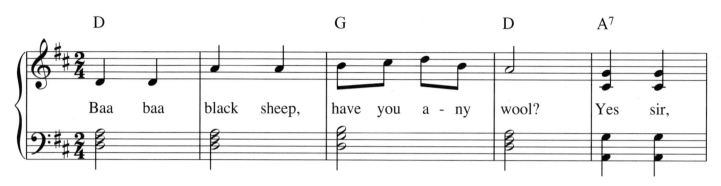

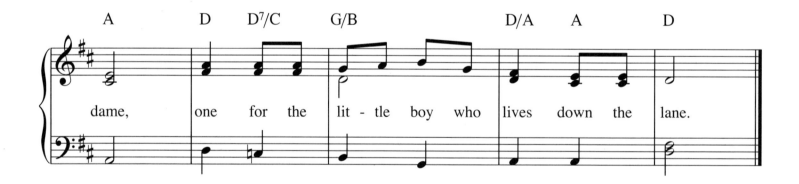

Baa baa black sheep, have you any wool?
Yes sir, yes sir, three bags full.
One for the master, one for the dame,
One for the little boy who lives down the lane.

Bobby Shaftoe

Traditional

Moderately

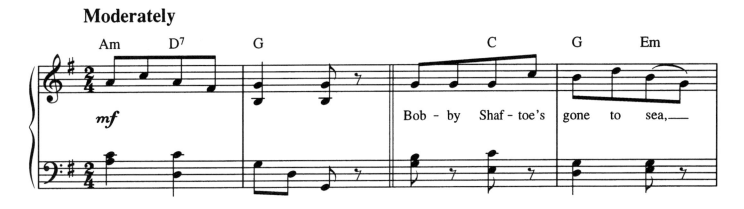

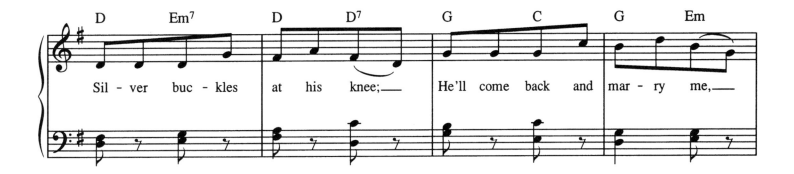

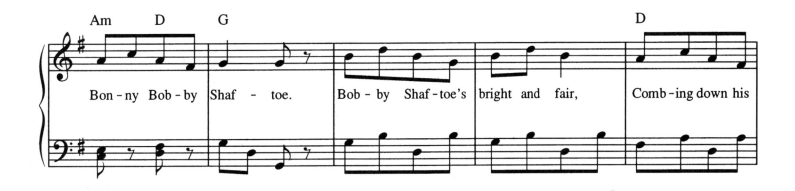

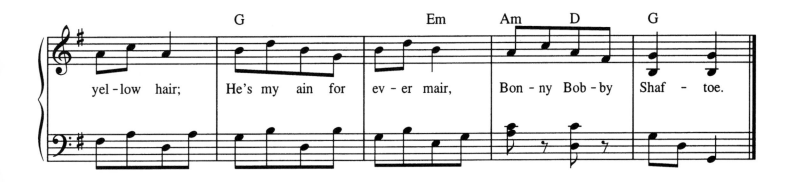

Blowing Bubbles

Traditional

Moderately

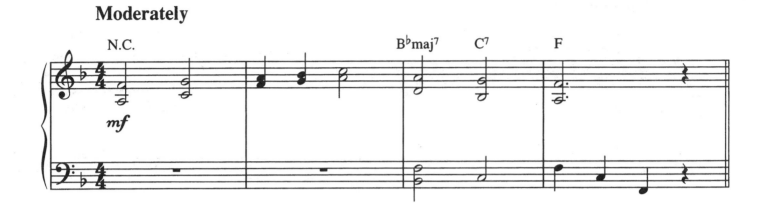

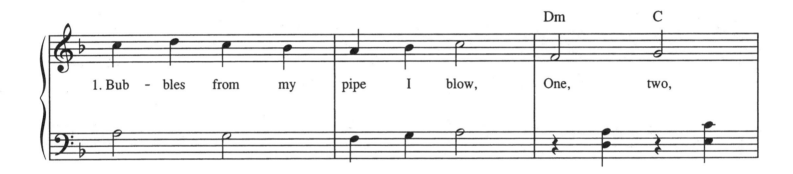

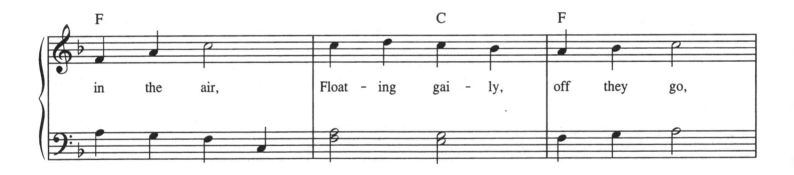

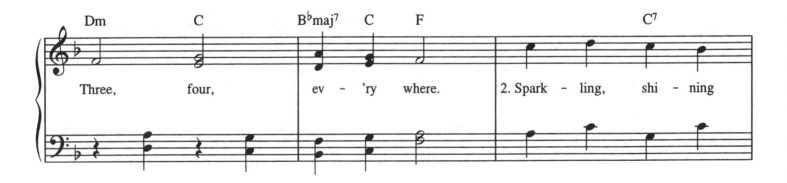

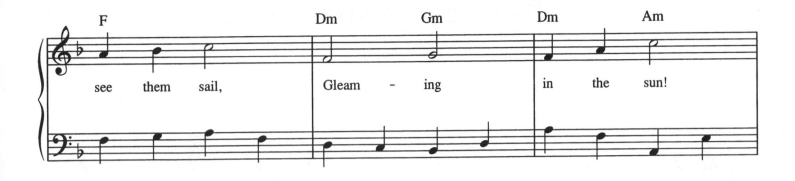

see them sail, Gleam - ing in the sun!

Air - y fair - y balls so frail, Rain - bows

in each one. *p*

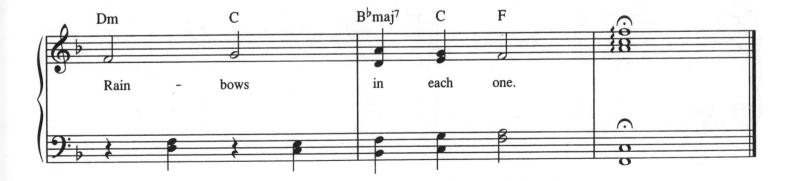

Rain - bows in each one.

Bye, Baby Bunting

Traditional

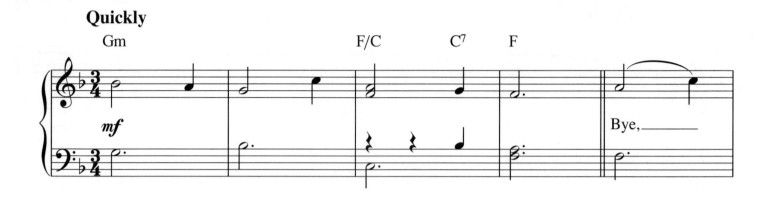

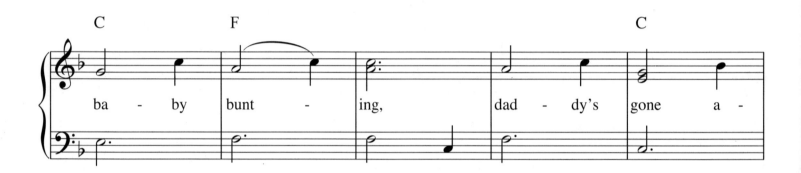

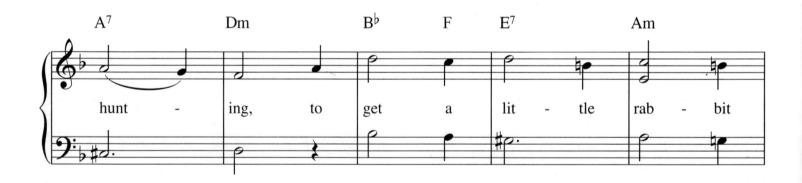

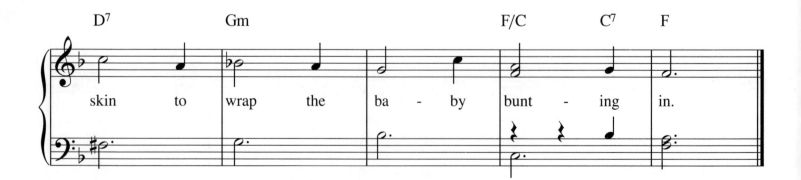

Curly Locks

Traditional

Gently

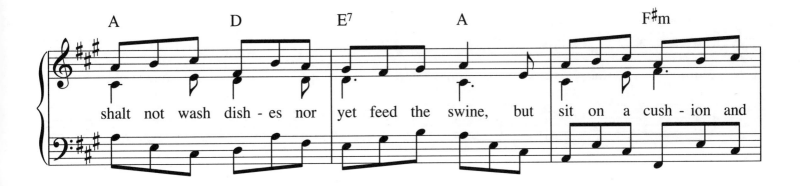

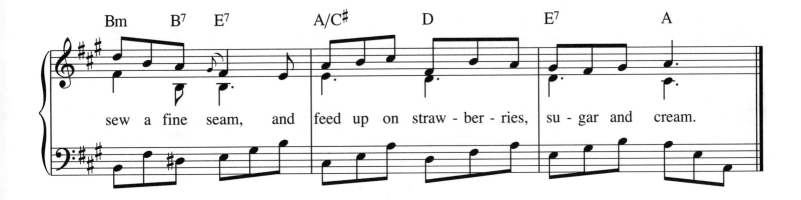

Curly Locks, Curly Locks, when thou be mine,
Thou shalt not wash dishes nor yet feed the swine,
But sit on a cushion and sew a fine seam,
And feed up on strawberries, sugar and cream.

Camptown Races

Words & Music by Stephen Collins Foster

Lively

Camp - town la - dies sing this song, doo - dah, doo - dah,

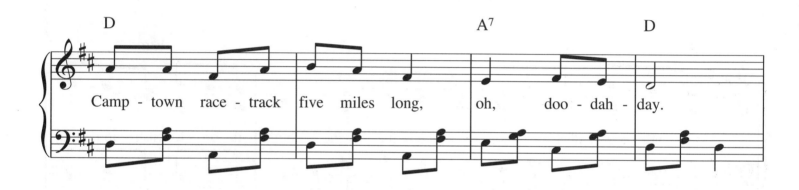

Camp - town race - track five miles long, oh, doo - dah - day.

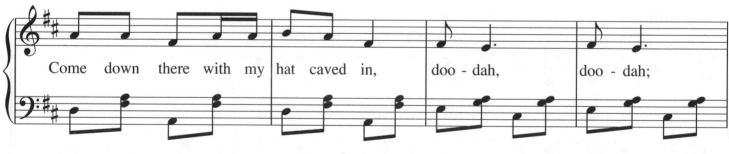

Come down there with my hat caved in, doo - dah, doo - dah;

Go back home with my pock - et full of tin, oh, doo - dah - day.

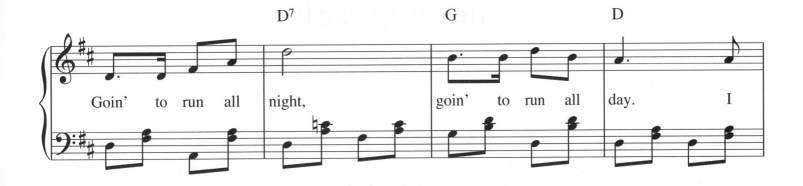

Verse 2:
The long-tail filly and the big black hoss,
Doo-dah, doo-dah,
Fly the track and they both cut across,
Oh, doo-dah-day.
The blind hoss shaken in a big mud hole,
Doo-dah, doo-dah,
Can't touch bottom with a ten-foot pole,
Oh, doo-dah-day.
Goin' to run all night, goin' to run all day.
I bet my money on the bobtail nag;
Somebody bet on the bay.

Verse 3:
Old muley cow came onto the track,
Doo-dah, doo-dah,
Bobtail fling her over his back,
Oh, doo-dah-day.
Then fly along like a railroad car,
Doo-dah, doo-dah,
Running a race with a shooting star,
Oh, doo-dah-day.
Goin' to run all night, goin' to run all day.
I bet my money on the bobtail nag;
Somebody bet on the bay.

Verse 4:
See the flying on a ten-mile heat,
Doo-dah, doo-dah,
'Round the racetrack, then repeat,
Oh, doo-dah-day.
I win my money on a bobtail nag,
Doo-dah, doo-dah,
Keep my money in an old tow bag,
Oh, doo-dah-day.
Goin' to run all night, goin' to run all day.
I bet my money on the bobtail nag;
Somebody bet on the bay.

Chook Chook

Traditional

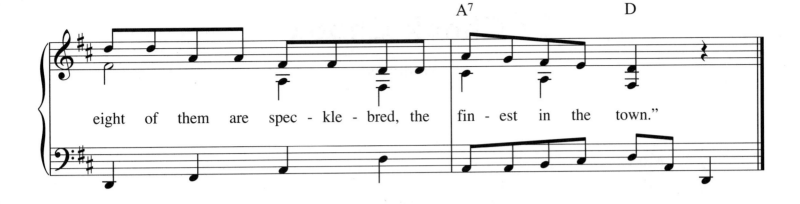

eight of them are spec - kle - bred, the fin - est in the town."

Verse 2:
Chook, chook, chook, chook, chook,
"Good morning Mrs Hen.
How many chickens have you got?"
"Madam, I've got ten.
Two of them are yellow,
And two of them are brown,
And six of them are speckle-bred,
The finest in the town."

Verse 3:
Chook, chook, chook, chook, chook,
"Good morning Mrs Hen.
How many chickens have you got?"
"Madam, I've got ten.
Three of them are yellow,
And three of them are brown,
And four of them are speckle-bred,
The finest in the town."

Verse 4:
Chook, chook, chook, chook, chook,
"Good morning Mrs Hen.
How many chickens have you got?"
"Madam, I've got ten.
Four of them are yellow,
And four of them are brown,
And two of them are speckle-bred,
The finest in the town."

Verse 5:
Chook, chook, chook, chook, chook,
"Good morning Mrs Hen.
How many chickens have you got?"
"Madam, I've got ten.
Five of them are yellow,
And five of them are brown,
And none of them are speckle-bred,
The finest in the town."

Cock-A-Doodle-Doo

Traditional

Cock - a - doo - dle - doo, my dame has lost her shoe. My

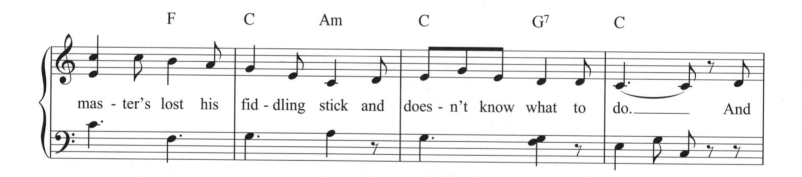

mas - ter's lost his fid - dling stick and does - n't know what to do. _____ And

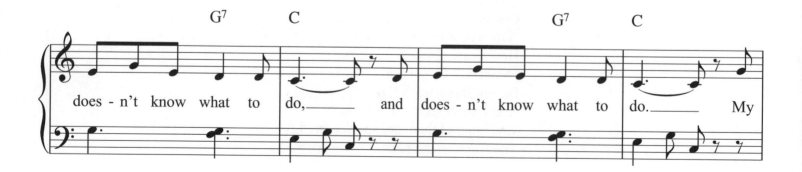

does - n't know what to do, _____ and does - n't know what to do. _____ My

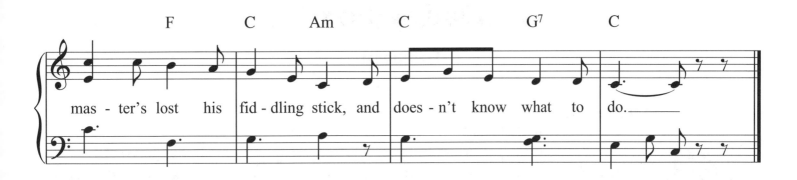

mas - ter's lost his fid - dling stick, and does-n't know what to do._____

Verse 2:
Cock-a-doodle doo, what is my dame to do?
'Til master finds his fiddling stick,
She'll dance without her shoe.
She'll dance without her shoe,
She'll dance without her shoe.
'Til master finds his fiddling stick,
She'll dance without her shoe.

Doctor Foster

Traditional

Moderately

mf Doc - tor Fos - ter went_ to Glouces - ter in a show - er of rain;_____ he

stepped in a pud - dle, right up to his mid - dle, and nev - er went there a - gain.

Daddy Fox

Traditional

With movement

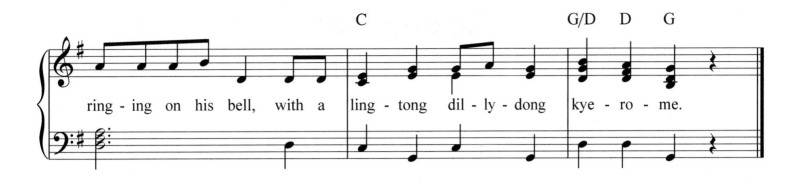

ring - ing on his bell, with a ling - tong dil - ly - dong kye - ro - me.

Chorus:
Hey! Fa-la-le, fa-la-la,
Fa-la-lay-ro.
Hey! Fa-la-lay-ro, lay-ro-lee.
Up jumps John,
Ringing on his bell,
With a ling-tong dilly-dong kye-ro-me.

Verse 2:
Well, he ran 'til he came to a great big pen,
With a ling-tong dilly-dong kye-ro-me;
And the ducks and the geese were kept therein,
With a ling-tong dilly-dong kye-ro-me.

Hey! Fa-la-le, fa-la-la, *etc.*

Verse 3:
He grabbed the grey goose by the neck,
With a ling-tong dilly-dong kye-ro-me;
And up with the little ones over his back,
With a ling-tong dilly-dong kye-ro-me.

Hey! Fa-la-le, fa-la-la, *etc.*

Verse 4:
Old Mother Flipper-Flopper jumped out of bed,
With a ling-tong dilly-dong kye-ro-me;
Out of the window she stuck her little head,
With a ling-tong dilly-dong kye-ro-me.

Hey! Fa-la-le, fa-la-la, *etc.*

Verse 5:
John, he ran to the top hill,
With a ling-tong dilly-dong kye-ro-me;
And he blew his little horn both loud and shrill,
With a ling-tong dilly-dong kye-ro-me.

Hey! Fa-la-le, fa-la-la, *etc.*

Verse 6:
The fox, he ran to his cosy den,
With a ling-tong dilly-dong kye-ro-me;
And there were the little ones, eight, nine, ten,
With a ling-tong dilly-dong kye-ro-me.

Hey! Fa-la-le, fa-la-la, *etc.*

Verse 7:
Then the fox and his wife, without any strife,
With a ling-tong dilly-dong kye-ro-me;
They cut up the goose with a carving knife,
With a ling-tong dilly-dong kye-ro-me.

Hey! Fa-la-le, fa-la-la, *etc.*

Diddle, Diddle Dumpling, My Son John

Traditional

Diddle, diddle dumpling, my son John
Went to bed with his trousers on;
One shoe off, and one shoe on,
Diddle, diddle, dumpling, my son John.

Ding Dong Bell

Traditional

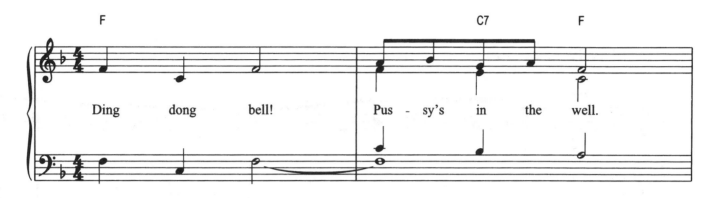

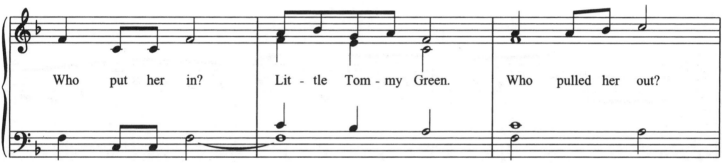

Do Your Ears Hang Low?

Traditional

1. Do your

ears hang low? Do they wob - ble to and fro? Can you tie 'em in a knot? Can you

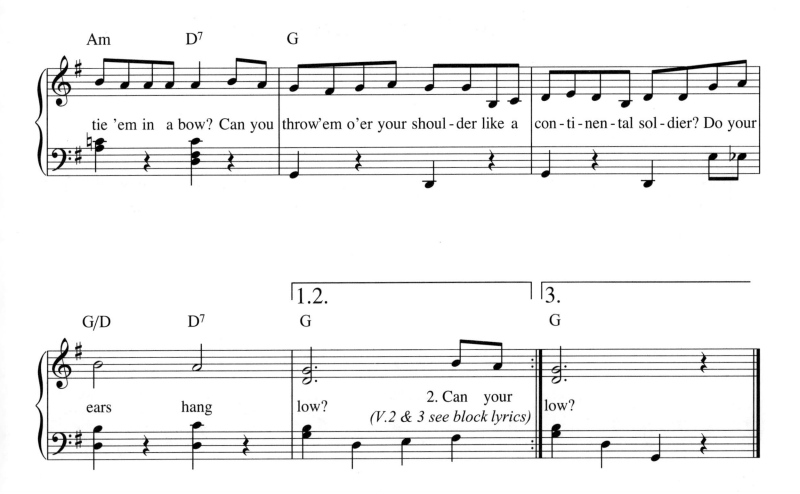

Verses 1 and 3:
Do your ears hang low?
Do they wobble to and fro?
Can you tie 'em in a knot?
Can you tie 'em in a bow?
Can you throw 'em o'er your shoulder like a continental soldier?
Do your ears hang low?

Verse 2:
Can your ears hang high?
Can they stand up to the sky?
Can they stand up if they're wet?
Can they stand up if they're dry?
Can you wave them to your neighbour with a minimum of labour?
Can your ears stand high?

Dry Bones

Traditional

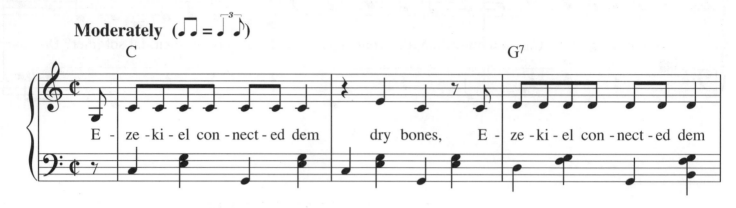

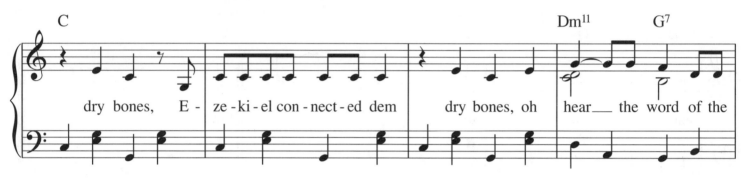

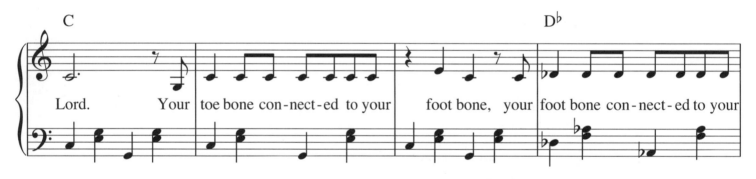

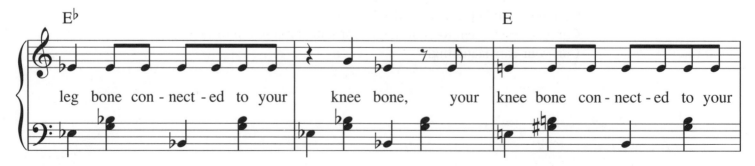

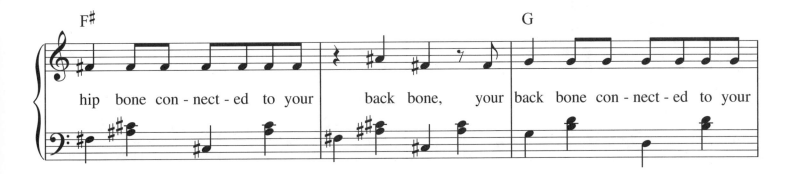

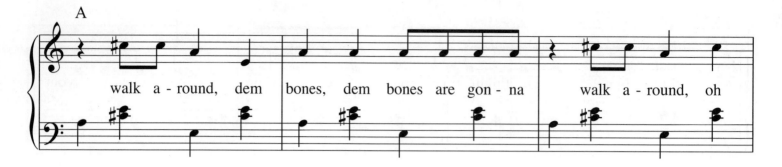

walk a - round, dem bones, dem bones are gon - na walk a - round, oh

hear___ the word of the Lord.___ Dis - con - nect dem bones, dem dry bones, dis - con -

- nect dem bones, dem dry bones, dis - con - nect dem bones, dem dry bones. Oh

hear___ the word of the Lord.___ Your head bone con - nect - ed to your

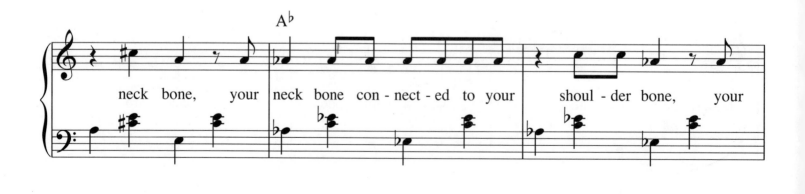

neck bone, your neck bone con - nect - ed to your shoul - der bone, your

shoul - der bone con - nect - ed to your | back bone, your | back bone con - nect - ed to your

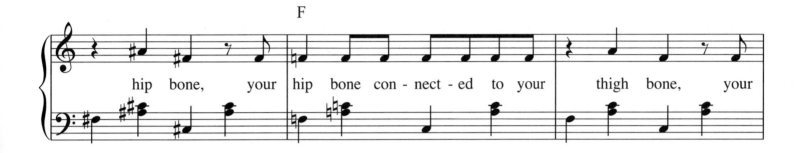

hip bone, your | hip bone con - nect - ed to your | thigh bone, your

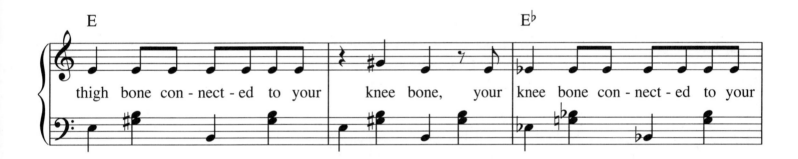

thigh bone con - nect - ed to your | knee bone, your | knee bone con - nect - ed to your

leg bone, your | leg bone con - nect - ed to your | ank - le bone, your

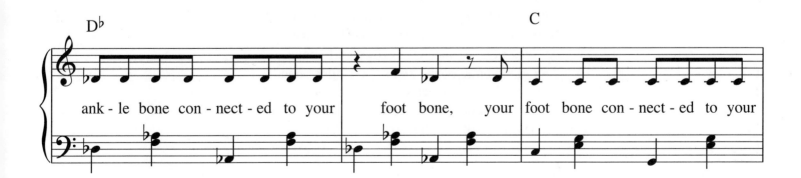

ank - le bone con - nect - ed to your | foot bone, your | foot bone con - nect - ed to your

toe bone, oh hear__ the word of the Lord. Oh hear__ the word of the Lord.

Ezekiel connected dem dry bones,
Ezekiel connected dem dry bones,
Ezekiel connected dem dry bones,
Oh hear the word of the Lord.

Your toe bone connected to your foot bone,
Your foot bone connected to your ankle bone,
Your ankle bone connected to your leg bone,
Your leg bone connected to your knee bone,
Your knee bone connected to your thigh bone,
Your thigh bone connected to your hip bone,
Your hip bone connected to your back bone,
Your back bone connected to your shoulder bone,
Your shoulder bone connected to your neck bone,
Your neck bone connected to your head bone,
Oh hear the word of the Lord.

Dem bones, dem bones are gonna walk around,
Dem bones, dem bones are gonna walk around,
Dem bones, dem bones are gonna walk around,
Oh hear the word of the Lord.

Disconnect dem bones, dem dry bones,
Disconnect dem bones, dem dry bones,
Disconnect dem bones, dem dry bones,
Oh hear the word of the Lord.

Your head bone connected to your neck bone,
Your neck bone connected to your shoulder bone,
Your shoulder bone connected to your back bone,
Your back bone connected to your hip bone,
Your hip bone connected to your thigh bone,
Your thigh bone connected to your knee bone,
Your knee bone connected to your leg bone,
Your leg bone connected to your ankle bone,
Your ankle bone connected to your foot bone,
Your foot bone connected to your toe bone,
Oh hear the word of the Lord.
Oh hear the word of the Lord.

Fiddle-De-Dee

Traditional

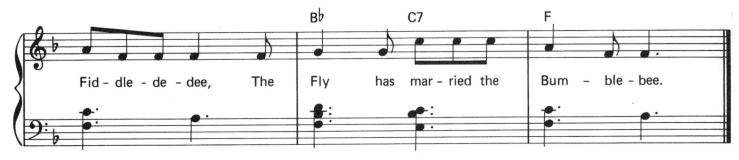

Verse 2:
Fiddle-dee-dee, fiddle-dee-dee,
The Fly has married the Bumblebee,
Says the Bee, says she, "I'll live under your wing,
And you'll never know I carry a sting."

Fiddle-dee-dee, *etc.*

Verse 3:
Fiddle-dee-dee, fiddle-dee-dee,
The Fly has married the Bumblebee,
And when parson Beetle had married the pair,
They both went out to take the air.

Fiddle-dee-dee, *etc.*

Eeensy Weensy Spider

Traditional

Moderately

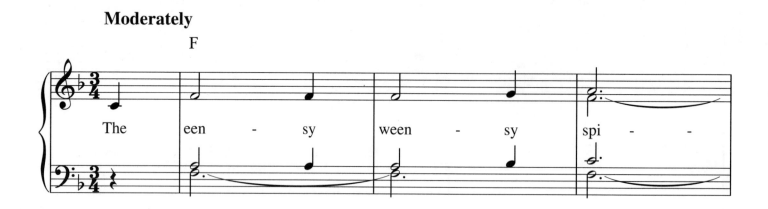

The een - sy ween - sy spi - -

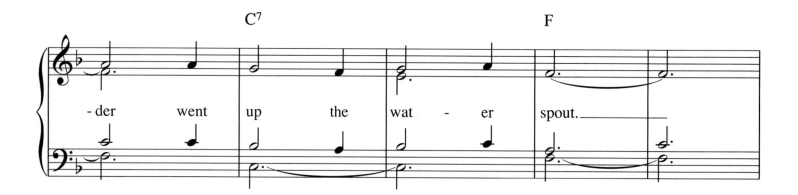

- der went up the wat - er spout.

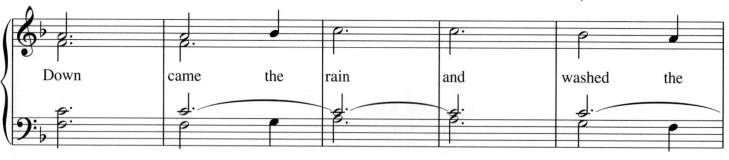

Down came the rain and washed the

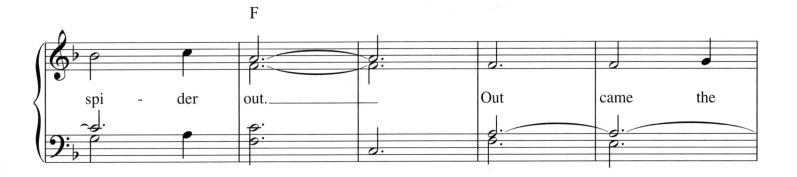

spi - der out._____ Out came the

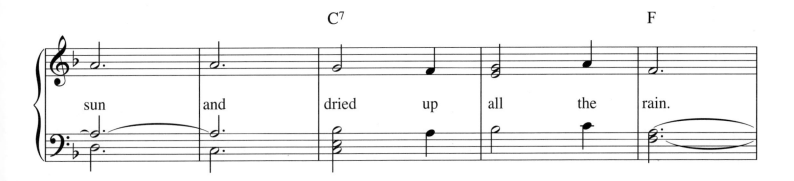

sun and dried up all the rain.

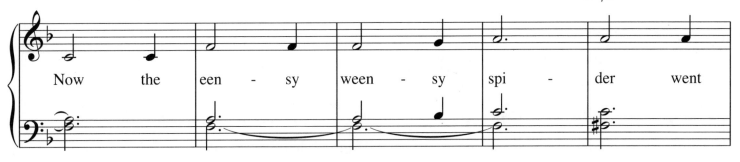

Now the een - sy ween - sy spi - der went

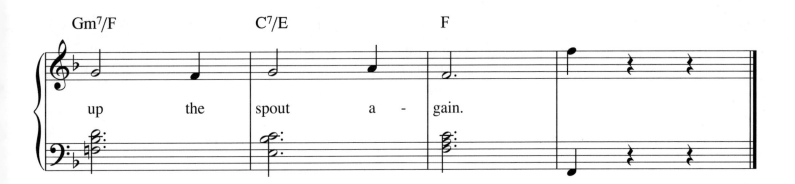

up the spout a - gain.

Fee! Fi! Foe! Fum!

Traditional

Slow and heavy

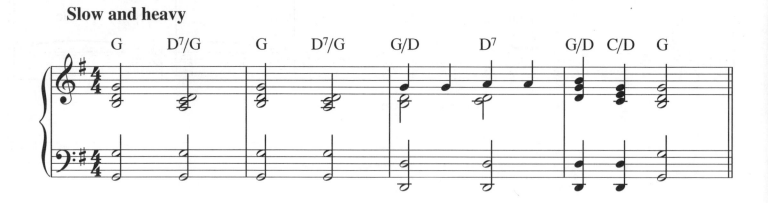

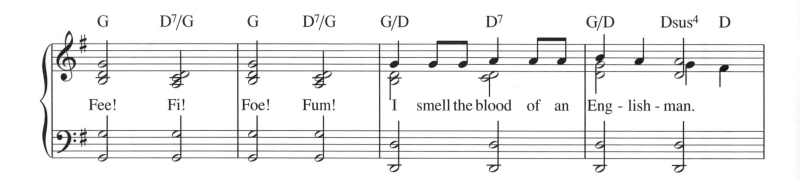

Fee! Fi! Foe! Fum!
I smell the blood of an Englishman.
Be he 'live, or be he dead,
I'll grind his bones to make my bread.

Five Little Ducks

Traditional

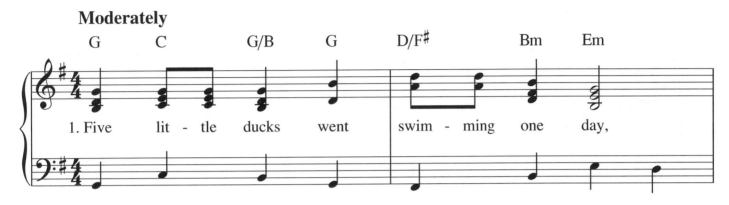

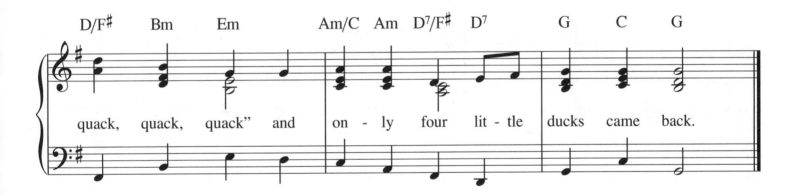

Verse 2:
Four little ducks went swimming one day, *etc.*

Verse 3:
Three little ducks went swimming one day, *etc.*

Verse 4:
Two little ducks went swimming one day, *etc.*

Verse 5:
One little duck went swimming one day,
Over the hills and far away.
The mother duck said, "Quack, quack, quack, quack"
And five little ducks came swimming right back.

Five Little Speckled Frogs

Traditional

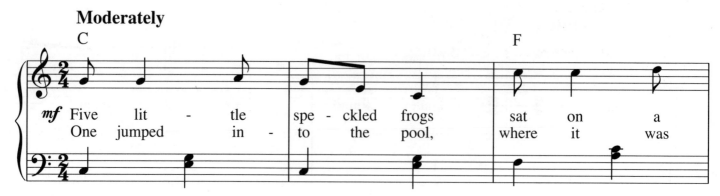

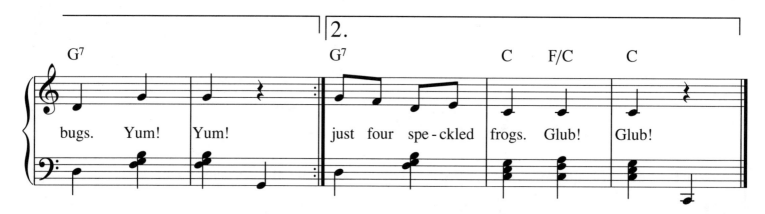

Verse 2:
Four little speckled frogs *etc.*

Verse 3:
Three little speckled frogs *etc.*

Verse 4:
Two little speckled frogs *etc.*

Verse 5:
One little speckled frog
Sat on a speckled log,
Eating some most delicious bugs,
Yum! Yum!
One jumped into the pool,
Where it was nice and cool,
Now there are no more speckled frogs,
Glub! Glub!

Found A Peanut

Traditional

Moderately

Found a pea - nut, found a pea - nut found a

pea - nut last___ night.   Last___ night I found a

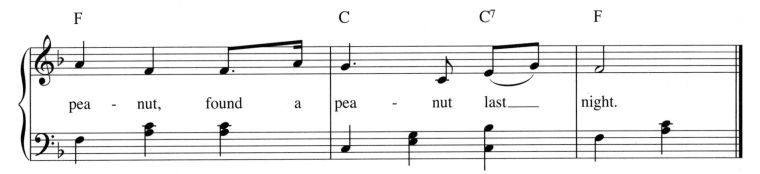

pea - nut, found a pea - nut last___ night.

Verse 2:
Where'd you find it? Where'd you find it?
Where'd you find it last night?
Last night, where'd you find it?
Where'd you find it last night?

Verse 3:
In a dustbin, *etc.*

Verse 4:
Cracked it open, *etc.*

Verse 5:
Found it rotten, *etc.*

Verse 6:
Ate it anyway, *etc.*

Verse 7:
I felt sick, *etc.*

Verse 8:
Called the doctor, *etc.*

Verse 9:
Went to Heaven, *etc.*

Verse 10:
Didn't want me, *etc.*

Verse 11:
Went the other way, *etc.*

Verse 12:
Shovelling coal, *etc.*

Frog Went A-Courtin'

Traditional

Moderately

1. A frog went a-courtin' and he did ride, hmm-hmmm.

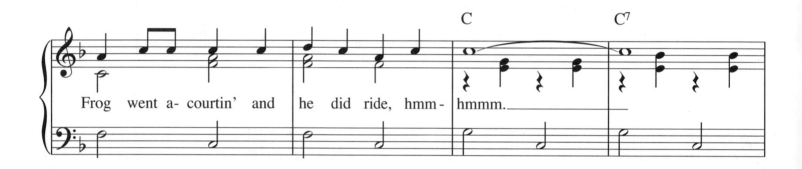

Frog went a-courtin' and he did ride, hmm-hmmm.

Frog went a-courtin' and he did ride, with a sword and a pis-tol

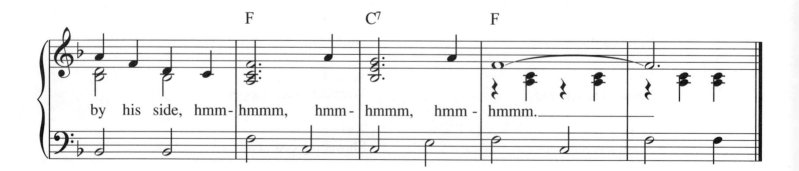

by his side, hmm-hmmm, hmm-hmmm, hmm-hmmm.

Verse 2:
Rode right up to Miss Mouse's door, hmm-hmmm.
Rode right up to Miss Mouse's door, hmm-hmmm.
Rode right up to Miss Mouse's door,
Gave three raps and a very loud roar,
Hmm-hmmm, hmm-hmmm, hmm-hmmm.

Verse 3:
Took Miss Mouse upon his knee, hmm-hmmm.
Took Miss Mouse upon his knee, hmm-hmmm.
Took Miss Mouse upon his knee,
Said, "Miss Mouse, will you marry me?"
Hmm-hmmm, hmm-hmmm, hmm-hmmm.

Verse 4:
"Where shall the wedding breakfast be?" Hmm-hmmm.
"Where shall the wedding breakfast be?" Hmm-hmmm.
"Where shall the wedding breakfast be?"
"Down in the swamp in the hollow tree."
Hmm-hmmm, hmm-hmmm, hmm-hmmm.

Verse 5:
"What shall the wedding breakfast be?" Hmm-hmmm.
"What shall the wedding breakfast be?" Hmm-hmmm.
"What shall the wedding breakfast be?"
"Fried mosquito and a black-eyed pea."
Hmm-hmmm, hmm-hmmm, hmm-hmmm.

Frère Jacques

Traditional

Moderately

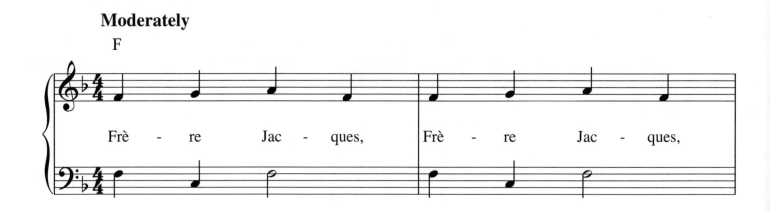

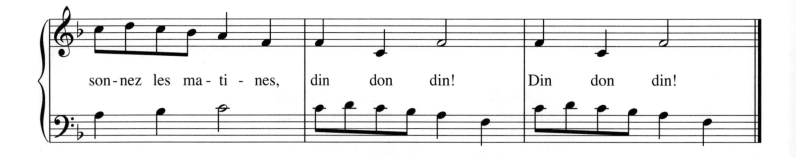

Frère Jacques, Frère Jacques,
Dormez vous? Dormez vous?
Sonnez les matines, sonnez les matines,
Din don din! Din don din!

Georgie Porgie

Traditional

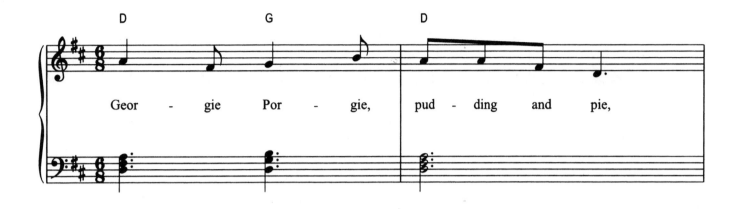

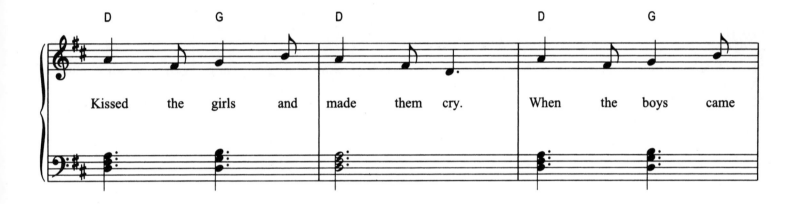

Georgie Porgie, pudding and pie,
Kissed the girls and made them cry.
When the boys came out to play,
Georgie Porgie ran away.

Ging Gang Gooli

Traditional

Lively, with bounce

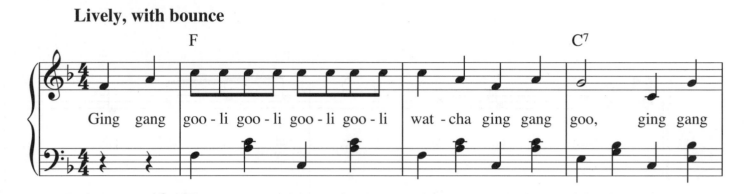

Ging gang goo - li goo - li goo - li goo - li wat - cha ging gang goo, ging gang

goo. Ging gang goo - li goo - li goo - li goo - li wat - cha ging gang goo, ging gang

goo! Hey - la, oh hey - la shey - la,

oh hey - la shey - la hey - la hoo.

Hey - la,_____ oh hey - la shey - la,_____ oh hey - la

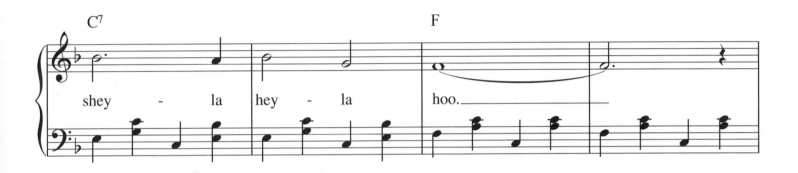

shey - la hey - la hoo._____

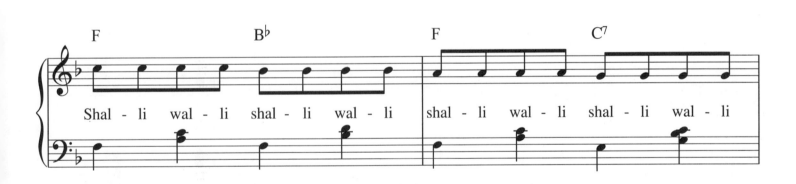

Shal - li wal - li shal - li wal - li shal - li wal - li shal - li wal - li

oom - pah oom - pah oom - pah oom - pah oom - pah oom - pah pah.

Going Over The Sea

Traditional

With a lilt

1. When I was one I played a drum, go - ing ov - er the

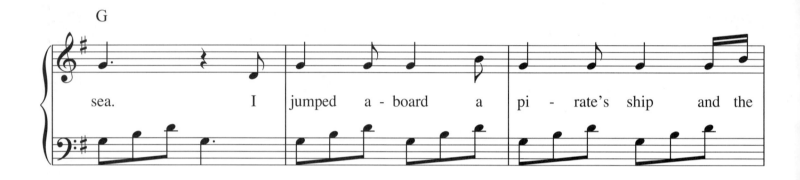

sea. I jumped a - board a pi - rate's ship and the

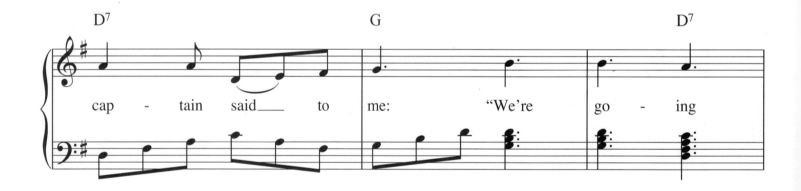

cap - tain said to me: "We're go - ing

this way, that way, for - wards and back - wards ov - er the Ir - ish

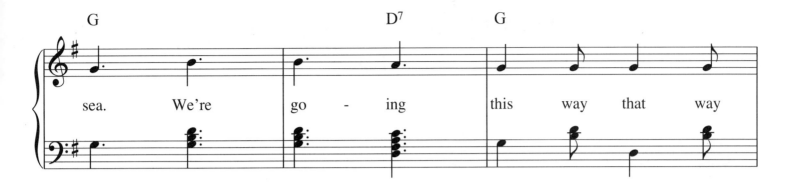

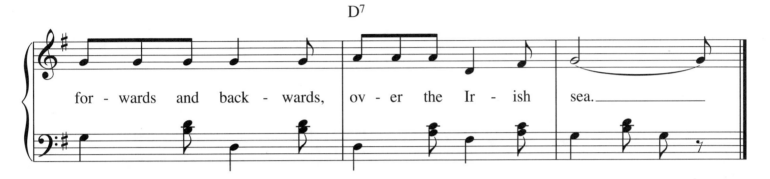

Chorus:
"We're going this way, that way, forwards and backwards
Over the Irish sea."
"We're going this way, that way, forwards and backwards
Over the Irish sea."

Verse 2:
When I was two I played a kazoo,
Going over the sea.
I jumped aboard a pirate's ship
And the captain said to me:

We're going this way, *etc.*

Verse 3:
When I was three I sang merrily,
Going over the sea.
I jumped aboard a pirate's ship
And the captain said to me:

We're going this way, *etc.*

Verse 4:
When I was four I danced on the floor,
Going over the sea.
I jumped aboard a pirate's ship
And the captain said to me:

We're going this way, *etc.*

Verse 5:
When I was five I did a jive,
Going over the sea.
I jumped aboard a pirate's ship
And the captain said to me:

We're going this way, *etc.*

Grandfather's Clock

Words & Music by Henry Clay Work

Lively

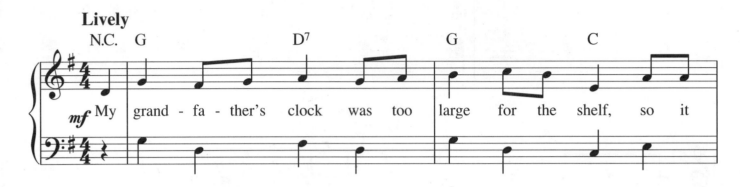

My grand-fa-ther's clock was too large for the shelf, so it

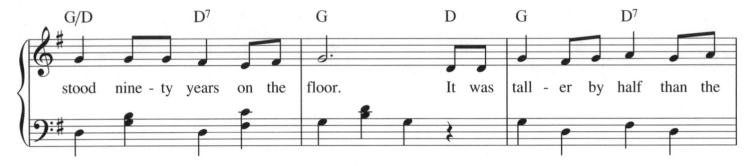

stood nine-ty years on the floor. It was tall-er by half than the

old man him-self, tho' it weighed not a pen-ny-weight more. It was

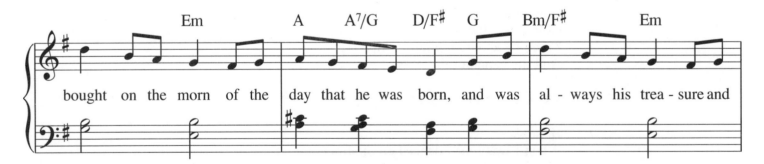

bought on the morn of the day that he was born, and was al-ways his trea-sure and

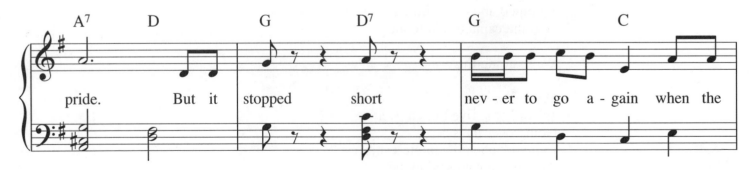

pride. But it stopped short nev-er to go a-gain when the

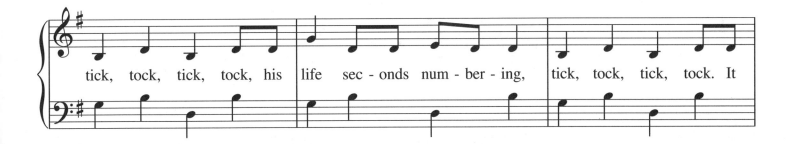

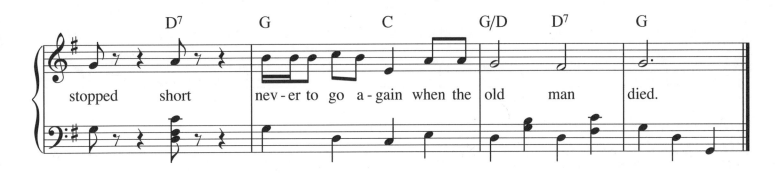

Chorus:
But it stopped short never to go again
When the old man died.
Ninety years without slumbering,
Tick, tock, tick, tock,
His life seconds numbering,
Tick, tock, tick, tock,
It stopped short never to go again
When the old man died.

Verse 2:
In watching its pendulum swing to and fro,
Many hours had he spent while a boy;
And in childhood and manhood the clock seemed
   to know
And to share both his grief and his joy.
For it struck twenty-four when he entered at the door,
With a blooming and beautiful bride.

But it stopped short never to go again, *etc.*

Verse 3:
My grandfather said that of those he could hire,
Not a servant so faithful he found;
For it wasted no time, and had but one desire
At the close of each week to be wound.
And it kept in its place not a frown upon its face,
And its hands never hung by its side.

But it stopped short never to go again, *etc.*

Verse 4:
It rang an alarm in the dead of the night,
An alarm that for years had been dumb;
And we knew that his spirit was pluming for flight,
That his hour of departure had come.
Still the clock kept the time, with a soft and
   muffled chime,
As we silently stood by his side.

But it stopped short never to go again, *etc.*

Green Grow The Rashes, O

Traditional

Moderately

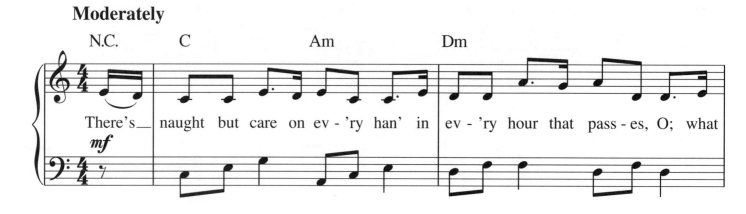

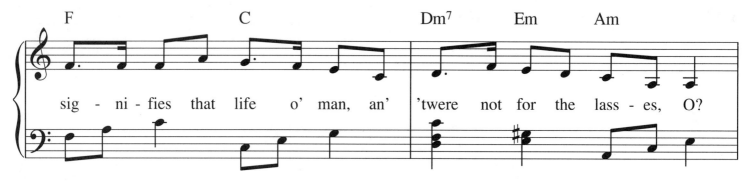

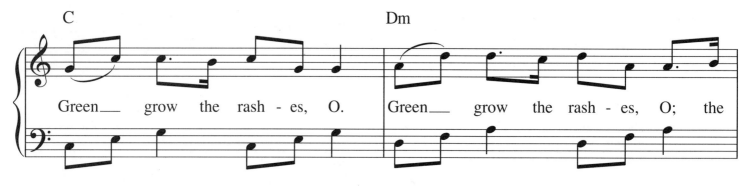

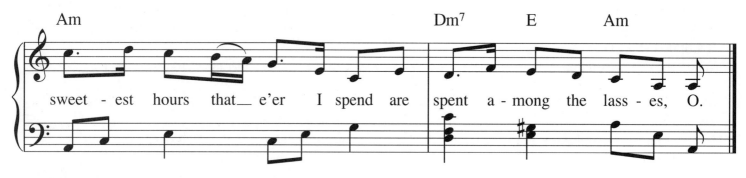

Chorus:
Green grow the rashes, O.
Green grow the rashes, O;
The sweetest hours that e'er I spend
Are spent among the lasses, O.

Verse 2:
The worldly race may riches chase,
An' riches still may fly them, O;
An' though at last they catch them fast,
Their hearts can ne'er enjoy them, O.

Green grow the rashes, O *etc.*

Verse 3:
Gie me a cannie hour at e'en,
My arms around my dearie, O;
An' worldly cares an' worldly men
May a' gae tapsalteerie, O!

Green grow the rashes, O *etc.*

Verse 4:
An' you sae douce, ye sneer at this,
Ye're naught but senseless asses, O;
The wisest man the world e'er saw,
He dearly loved the lasses, O.

Green grow the rashes, O *etc.*

Verse 5:
Auld nature swears the lovely dears,
Her noblest work she classes, O;
Her prentice han' she tried on man,
An' then she made the lasses, O.

Green grow the rashes, O *etc.*

Goosey, Goosey, Gander

Traditional

Have A Little Dog

Traditional

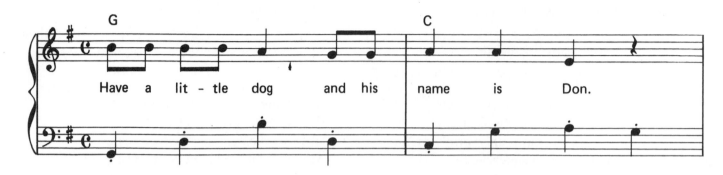

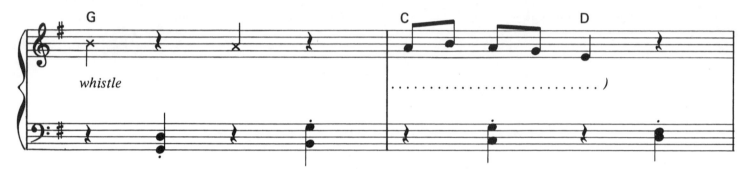

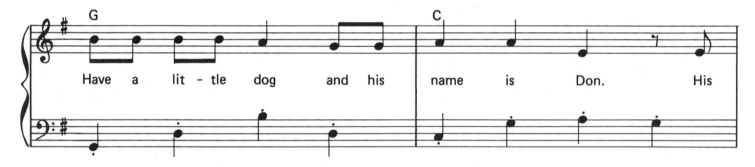

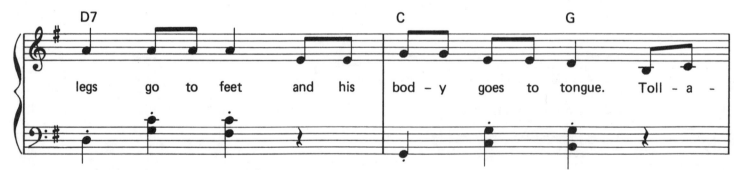

Verse 2:
Have a little box about three feet square, (whistle)
Have a little box about three feet square,
When I go to travel I put him in there,
Toll-a-winker, toll-a-winker, tum-tolly-aye.

Verse 3:
When I go to travel, I travel like an ox, (whistle)
When I go to travel, I travel like an ox,
And in that vest pocket I carry that box,
Toll-a-winker, toll-a-winker, tum-tolly-aye.

Verse 4:
Had a little hen and her colour was fair, (whistle)
Had a little hen and her colour was fair,
Sat her on a bomb and she hatched me a hare,
Toll-a-winker, toll-a-winker, tum-tolly-aye.

Verse 5:
The hare turned a horse about six feet high, (whistle)
The hare turned a horse about six feet high,
If you want to beat this you'll have to tell a lie,
Toll-a-winker, toll-a-winker, tum-tolly-aye.

Verse 6:
I had a little mule and his name was Jack, (whistle)
I had a little mule and his name was Jack,
I rode him on his tail to save his back,
Toll-a-winker, toll-a-winker, tum-tolly-aye.

Verse 7:
I had a little mule and his name was Jay, (whistle)
I had a little mule and his name was Jay,
I pulled his tail to hear him bray,
Toll-a-winker, toll-a-winker, tum-tolly-aye.

Verse 8:
I had a little mule, he was made of hay, (whistle)
I had a little mule, he was made of hay,
First big wind come along and blew him away,
Toll-a-winker, toll-a-winker, tum-tolly-aye.

Hark, Hark, The Dogs Do Bark

Traditional

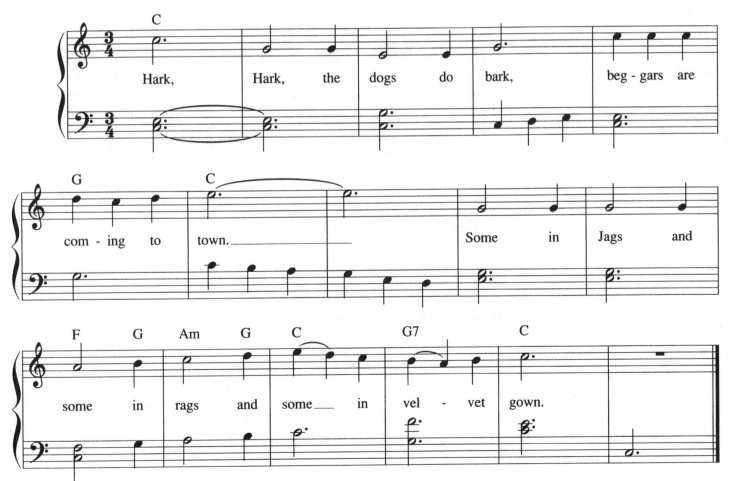

Head, Shoulders, Knees And Toes

Traditional

Head, shoulders, knees and toes,
Knees and toes.
Head, shoulders, knees and toes,
Knees and toes
And eyes and ears and mouth and nose.
Head, shoulders, knees and toes, knees and toes.

Activity:
Repeat the song, each time omitting a body part, in the order that they are sung. For example, the second time around you would point at your head but not actually say the word "head" out loud. The third time around you would leave out "head" and "shoulders" but still point to them. Keep doing this until you are not actually saying anything – just pointing at the body parts. You could also try getting faster and faster for an extra challenge!

Here We Go Gathering Nuts In May

Traditional

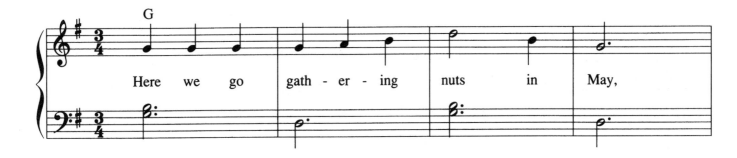

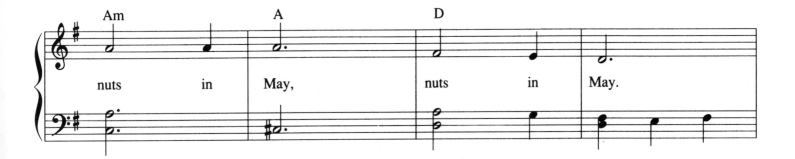

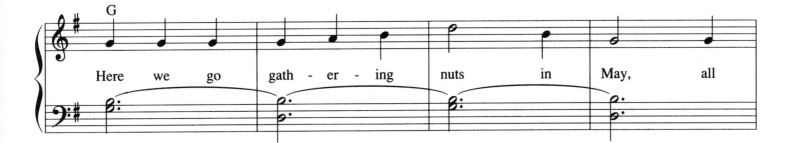

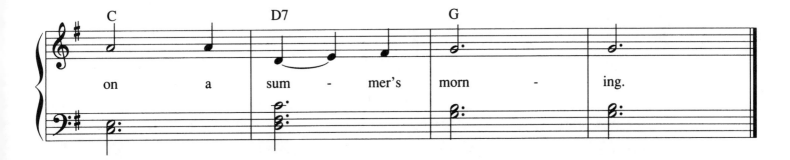

Verse 2:
Who will you have for nuts in May? *etc.*

Verse 3:
We'll have _____ for nuts in May. *etc.*

Verse 4:
Who will you send to fetch her/him away? *etc.*

Verse 5:
We'll send _____ to fetch her/him away. *etc.*

Here We Go Looby Loo

Traditional

With movement

Here we go loo - by loo, here we go loo - by light, here we go loo - by loo, all on a Sat - ur - day night.

1. Put your right hand in, put your right hand out, put your right hand in a - gain and shake it all_ a - bout.

Chorus:
Here we go looby loo,
Here we go looby light,
Here we go looby loo,
All on a Saturday night.

Verse 2:
Put your left hand in, *etc.*

Verse 3:
Put your right arm in, *etc.*

Verse 4:
Put your left arm in, *etc.*

Verse 5:
Put your right foot in, *etc.*

Verse 6:
Put your left foot in, *etc.*

Verse 7:
Put your right leg in, *etc.*

Verse 8:
Put your left leg in, *etc.*

Verse 9:
Put your back in, *etc.*

Verse 10:
Put your front in, *etc.*

Verse 11:
Put your head in, *etc.*

Verse 12:
Put your whole self in, *etc.*

Here We Go 'Round The Mulberry Bush

Traditional

With movement

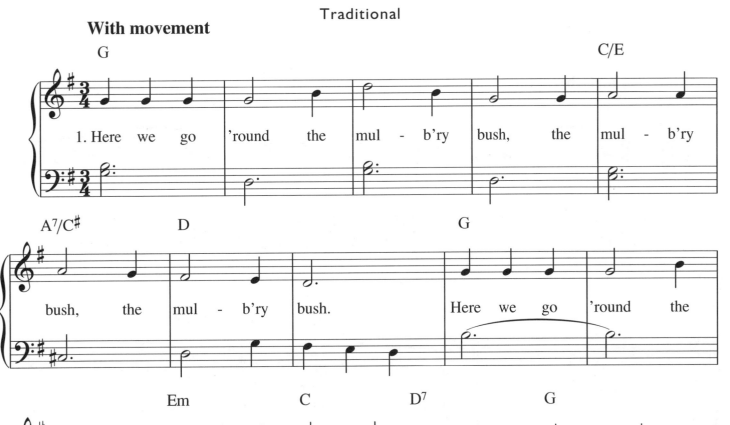

Verse 2:
This is the way we wash our hands,
We wash our hands, we wash our hands;
This is the way we wash our hands,
On a cold and frosty morning.

Verse 3:
This is the way we wash our clothes,
We wash our clothes, we wash our clothes;
This is the way we wash our clothes,
On a cold and frosty morning.

Verse 4:
This is the way we dry our clothes,
We dry our clothes, we dry our clothes;
This is the way we dry our clothes,
On a cold and frosty morning.

Verse 5:
This is the way we iron our clothes,
We iron our clothes, we iron our clothes;
This is the way we iron our clothes,
On a cold and frosty morning.

Verse 6:
This is the way we sweep the floor,
We sweep the floor, we sweep the floor;
This is the way we sweep the floor,
On a cold and frosty morning.

Verse 7:
This is the way we brush our hair,
We brush our hair, we brush our hair;
This is the way we brush our hair,
On a cold and frosty morning.

Verse 8:
This is the way we go to school,
We go to school, we go to school;
This is the way we go to school,
On a cold and frosty morning.

Verse 9:
This is the way we come back from school,
We come back from school, we come back from school;
This is the way we come back from school,
On a cold and frosty morning.

Hickory, Dickory Dock

Traditional

Fairly bright

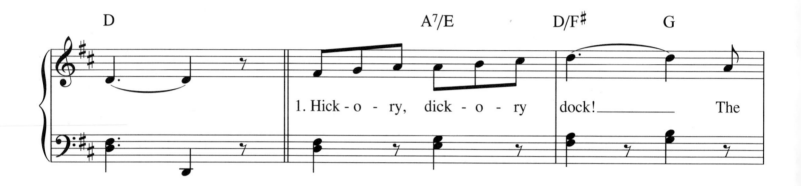

1. Hick - o - ry, dick - o - ry dock!_____ The

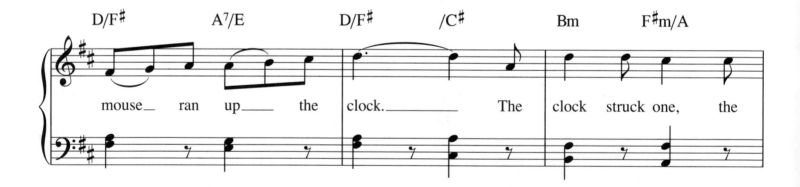

mouse___ ran up___ the clock._____ The clock struck one, the

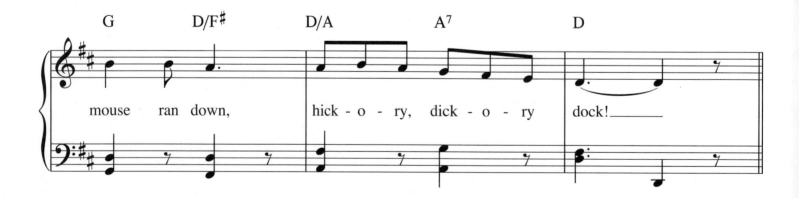

mouse ran down, hick - o - ry, dick - o - ry dock!_____

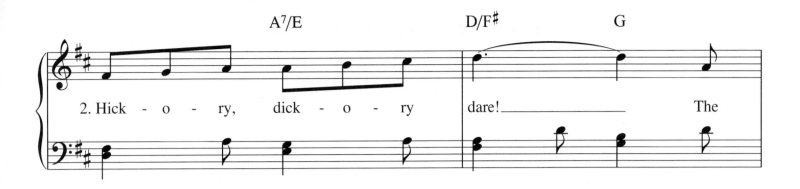

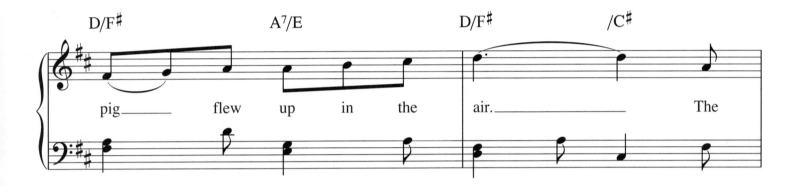

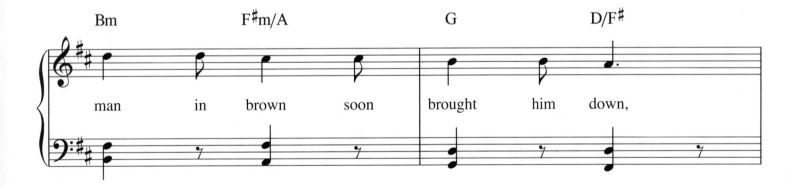

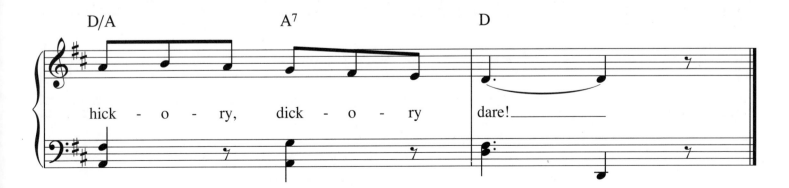

Hey Diddle Diddle

Traditional

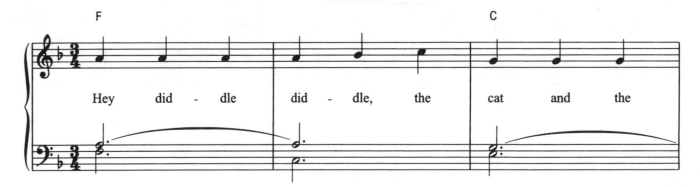

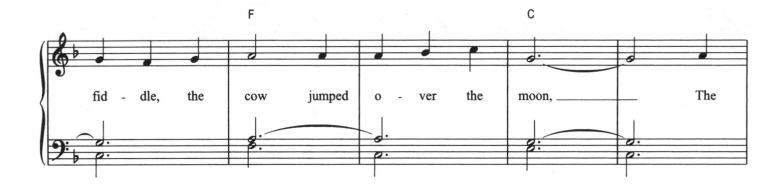

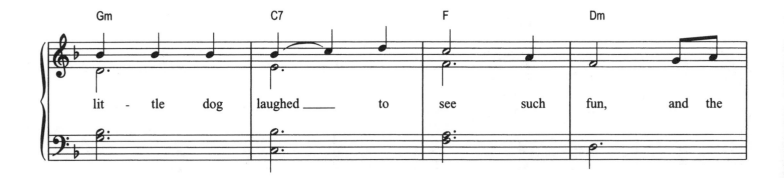

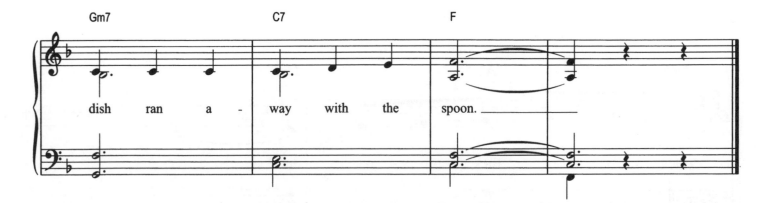

Hob Shoe Hob

Traditional

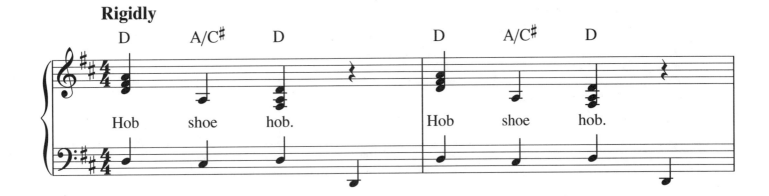

Hob shoe hob. Hob shoe hob.

Here a nail and there a nail and that's well shod.

Hob shoe hob.
Hob shoe hob.
Here a nail and there a nail
And that's well shod.

Hot Cross Buns

Traditional

Moderately bright

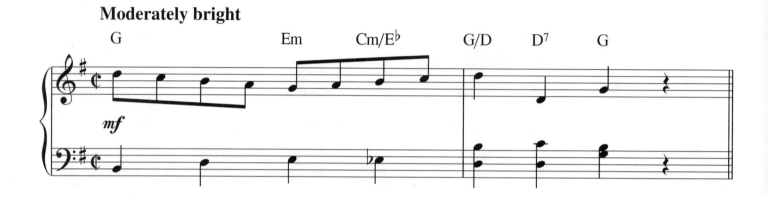

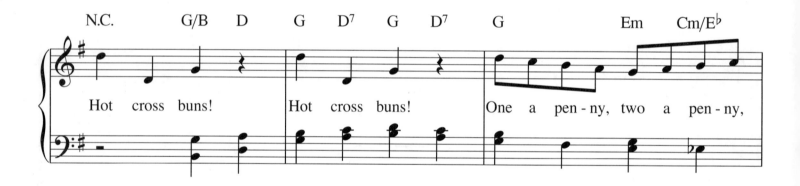

Hot cross buns! Hot cross buns! One a pen-ny, two a pen-ny,

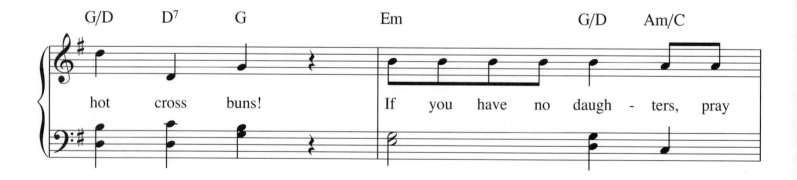

hot cross buns! If you have no daugh-ters, pray

give them to your sons,   one a pen-ny, two a pen-ny,   hot cross buns!

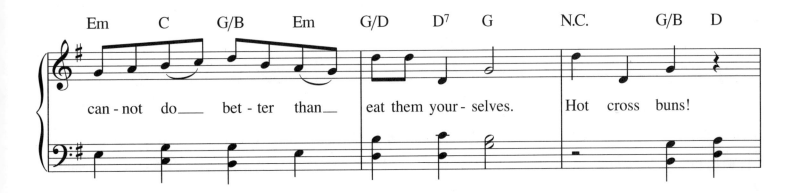

But   if   you   have   none   of   these   pret - ty   lit - tle   elves,   you

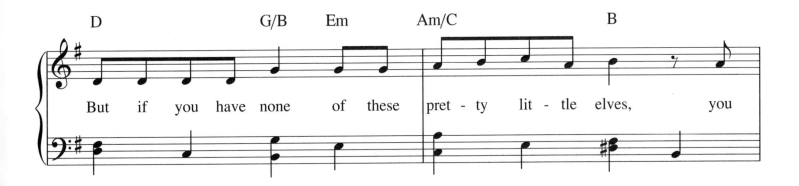

can - not   do___   bet - ter   than___   eat them your - selves.   Hot   cross   buns!

Hot   cross   buns!   One   a   pen - ny,   two   a   pen - ny,   hot   cross   buns!

Humpty Dumpty

Traditional

Moderately

Hump – ty Dump – ty sat on a wall.

Hump – ty Dump – ty had a great fall. All the King's hor – ses and

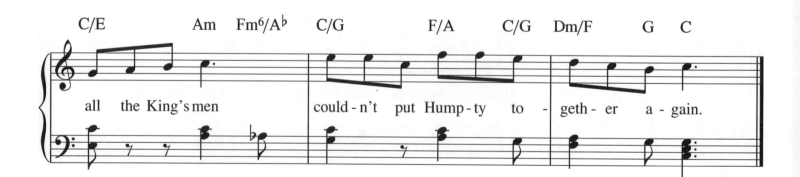

all the King's men could – n't put Hump – ty to – geth – er a – gain.

Hush-A-Bye, Baby

Traditional

Moderately

Hush - a - bye, Ba - by,

on the tree top, When the wind blows the cra - dle will rock.

When the bough breaks the cra - dle will fall, Down will come ba - by,

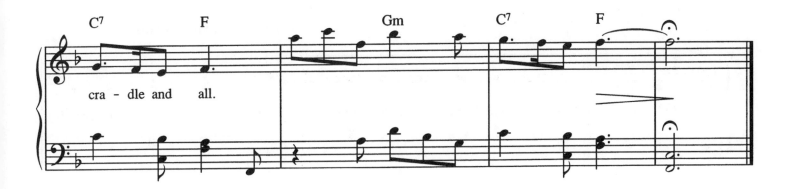

cra - dle and all.

Hush, Little Baby

Traditional

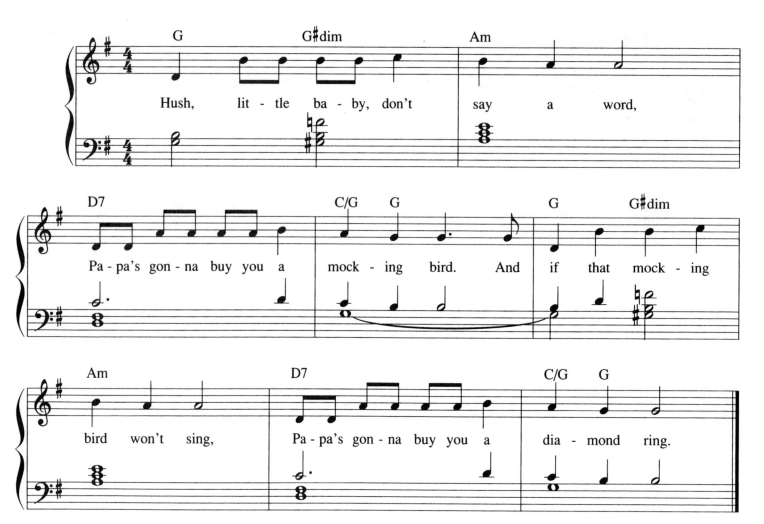

Hush, lit-tle ba-by, don't say a word, Pa-pa's gon-na buy you a mock-ing bird. And if that mock-ing bird won't sing, Pa-pa's gon-na buy you a dia-mond ring.

If You're Happy And You Know It

Traditional

If you're hap-py and you know it, clap your hands, if you're

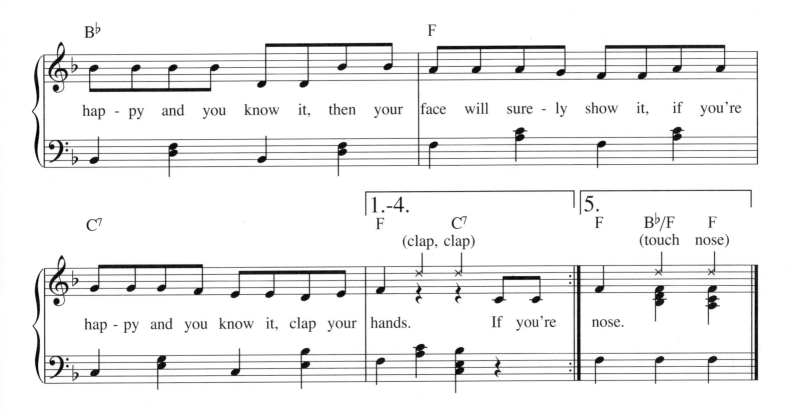

Verse 2:
If you're happy and you know it, stamp your feet,
(stamp, stamp)
If you're happy and you know it, stamp your feet,
(stamp, stamp)
If you're happy and you know it,
Then your face will surely show it,
If you're happy and you know it, stamp your feet.
(stamp, stamp)

Verse 3:
If you're happy and you know it, nod your head,
(nod, nod)
If you're happy and you know it, nod your head,
(nod, nod)
If you're happy and you know it,
Then your face will surely show it,
If you're happy and you know it, nod your head.
(nod, nod)

Verse 4:
If you're happy and you know it, turn around,
(turn around)
If you're happy and you know it, turn around,
(turn around)
If you're happy and you know it,
Then your face will surely show it,
If you're happy and you know it, turn around.
(turn around)

Verse 5:
If you're happy and you know it, touch your nose,
(touch nose)
If you're happy and you know it, touch your nose,
(touch nose)
If you're happy and you know it,
Then your face will surely show it,
If you're happy and you know it, touch your nose.
(touch nose)

I Had A Little Nut Tree

Traditional

I had a lit - tle nut tree noth - ing would it bear, but a sil - ver nut - meg and a gol - den pear. The King of Spain's daugh - ter came to vis - it me, and all ___ for the sake of my lit - tle nut tree.

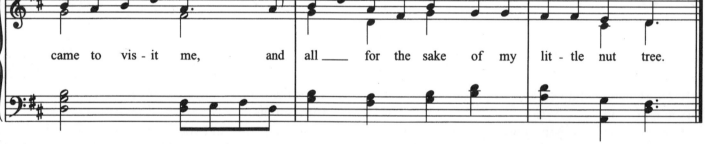

Verse 2:
I had a little nut tree,
Nothing would it bear,
But a silver nutmeg and a golden pear.
I skipped over water,
I danced over sea,
And all the birds in the air
Couldn't catch me.

I Love Little Pussy

Traditional

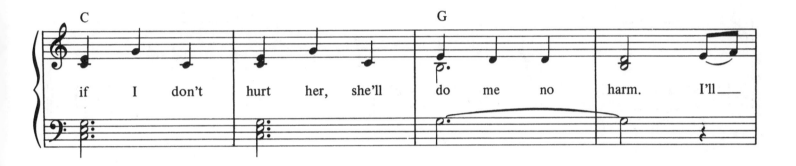

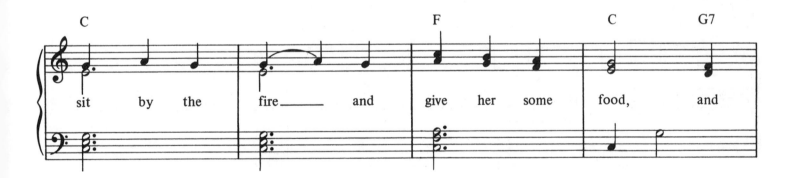

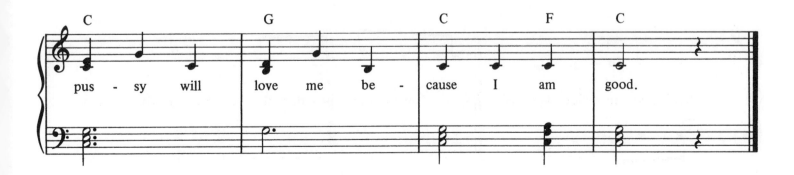

I Know An Old Lady
Who Swallowed A Fly

Traditional

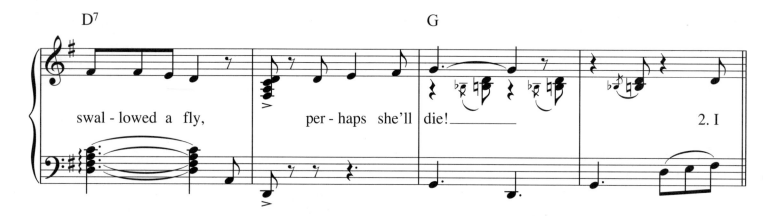

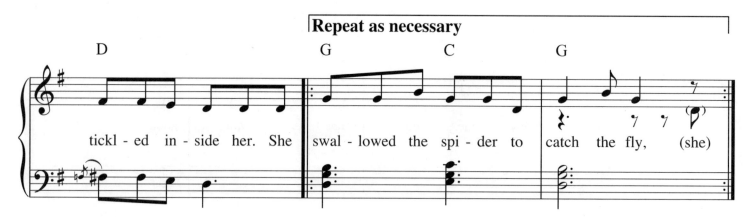

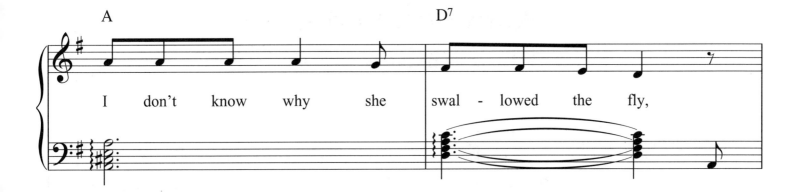

Fine **D.S. al Fine**

Verse 3:
I know an old lady who swallowed a bird.
How absurd, to swallow a bird!
She swallowed the bird to catch the spider
That wriggled and jiggled and tickled inside her.
She swallowed the spider to catch the fly,
I don't know why she swallowed a fly,
Perhaps she'll die!

Verse 4:
I know an old lady who swallowed a cat,
Just fancy that, she swallowed a cat!
She swallowed the cat to catch the bird,
She swallowed the bird to catch the spider, *etc.*

Verse 5:
I know an old lady who swallowed a dog,
What a hog, to swallow a dog!
She swallowed the dog to catch the cat,
She swallowed the cat to catch the bird, *etc.*

Verse 6:
I know an old lady who swallowed a goat.
She just opened her throat and swallowed a goat!
She swallowed the goat to catch the dog,
She swallowed the dog to catch the cat, *etc.*

Verse 7:
I know an old lady who swallowed a cow.
I don't know HOW she swallowed a cow.
She swallowed the cow to catch the goat,
She swallowed the goat to catch the dog, *etc.*

Verse 8:
I know an old lady who swallowed a rhinoceros,
THAT'S PREPOSTEROUS!!
She swallowed the rhino to catch the cow,
She swallowed the cow to catch the goat, *etc.*

Verse 9:
I know an old lady who swallowed a horse.
She's dead of course.

I'm A Nut

Traditional

Moderately

1. I'm a lit-tle a-corn, small and round ly-ing on the cold, cold ground. Peo-ple come and step on me, that's why I'm so cracked, you see! I'm a nut (click click), I'm a nut (click click), I'm a nut (click click), I'm a nut (click click).

Chorus:
I'm a nut (click click),
I'm a nut (click click),
I'm a nut (click click),
I'm a nut (click click).

Verse 2:
I love me, I think I'm grand,
I sit at the movies and hold my hand,
I put my arm around my waist
And when I get fresh, I slap my face.

Verse 3:
I call myself on the telephone
Just to hear my golden tone,
I ask myself for a little date
And pick myself up about half past eight.

It's Raining, It's Pouring

Traditional

Moderately

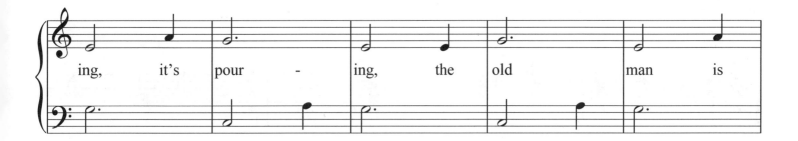

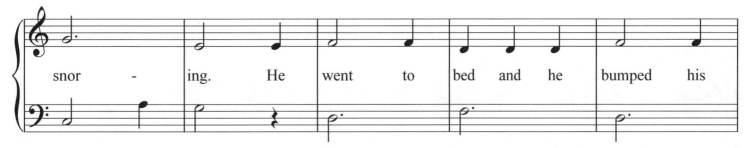

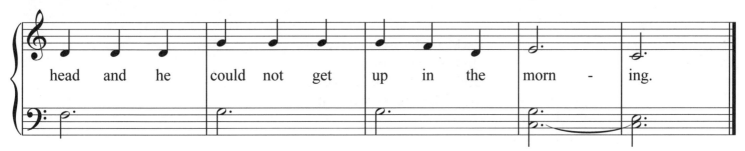

Jack And Jill

Traditional

Moderately

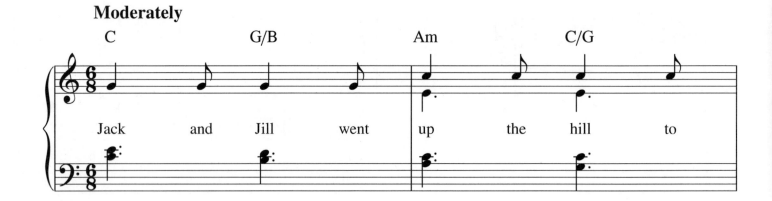

Jack and Jill went up the hill to

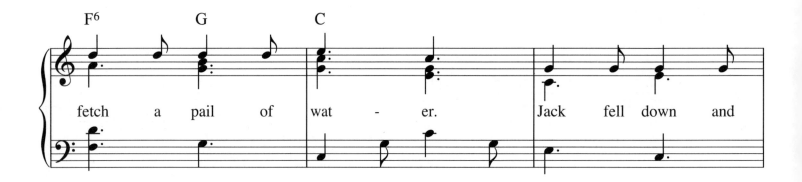

fetch a pail of wat - er. Jack fell down and

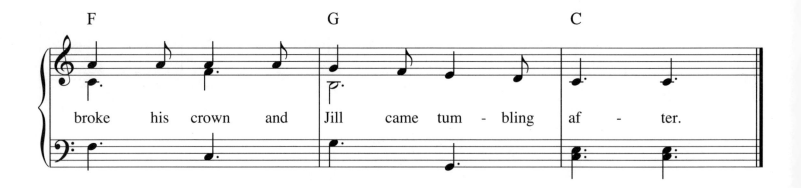

broke his crown and Jill came tum - bling af - ter.

Jack and Jill went up the hill,
To fetch a pail of water,
Jack fell down and broke his crown,
And Jill came tumbling after.

Jack Be Nimble

Traditional

79

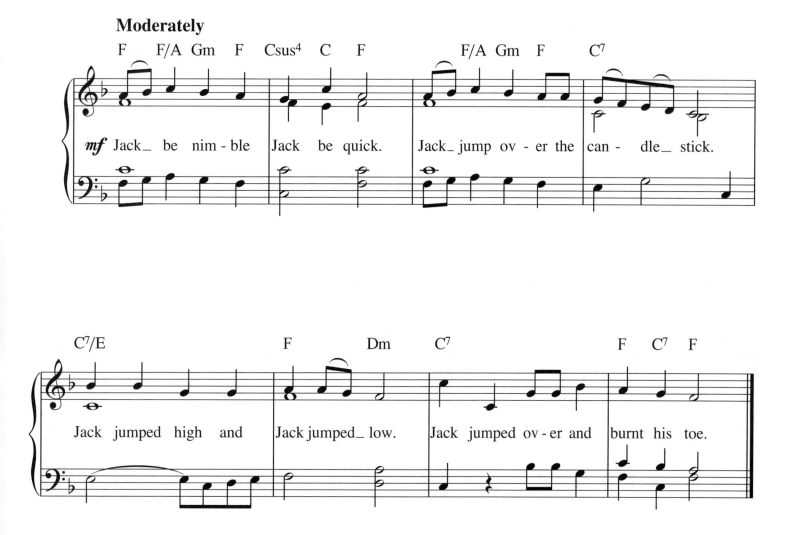

Jack be nimble, Jack be quick,
Jack jump over the candle stick.
Jack jumped high and Jack jumped low.
Jack jumped over and burnt his toe.

Jesus Loves Me

Music by William Batchfelder Bradbury
Words by Anna Warner

Steadily

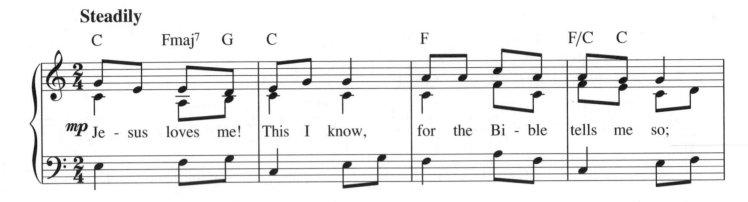

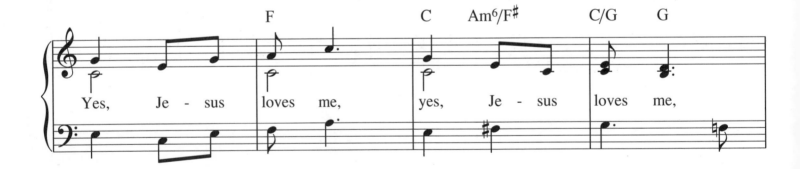

Kum Ba Yah

Traditional

Verse 2:
Someone's cryin', Lord, *etc.*

Verse 3:
Someone's singin', Lord, *etc.*

Verse 4:
Someone's shoutin', Lord, *etc.*

Knicky Knacky Knocky Noo

Traditional

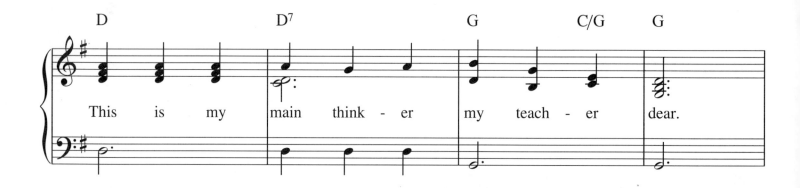

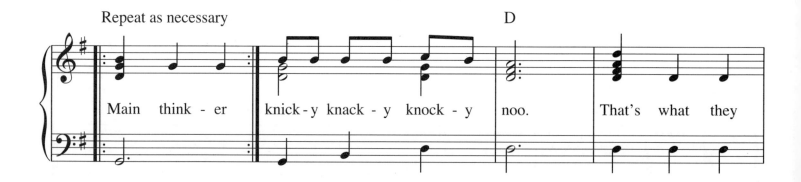

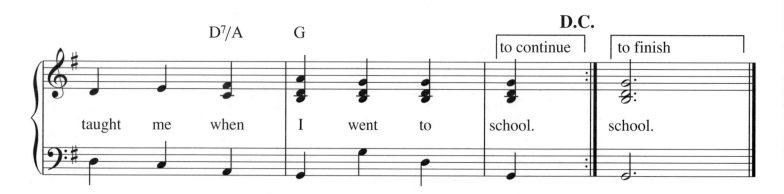

Verse 2:
With my hands on my eyes,
What have I here?
These are my eye peepers my teacher dear.
Main thinker, eye peepers, knicky knacky knocky noo.
That's what they taught me when I went to school.

Verse 3:
With my hands on my nose,
What have I here?
This is my smell boxer my teacher dear.
Main thinker, eye peepers, smell boxer, *etc.*

Verse 4:
With my hands on my mouth,
What have I here?
This is my chatterboxer, *etc.*

Verse 5:
With my hands on my chin,
What have I here?
This is my chin wagger, *etc.*

Verse 6:
With my hands on my chest,
What have I here?
This is my air blower, *etc.*

Verse 7:
With my hands on my stomach,
What have I here?
This is my bread basket, *etc.*

Verse 8:
With my hands on my lap,
What have I here?
This is my lap sitter, *etc.*

Verse 9:
With my hands on my knees,
What have I here?
These are my knee knockers, *etc.*

Verse 10:
With my hands on my feet,
What have I here?
These are my toe tappers, *etc.*

Ladybird, Ladybird

Traditional

La - dy - bird, la - dy - bird, fly a - way home, your house is on fire and your chil-dren all gone.

Lavender's Blue

Traditional

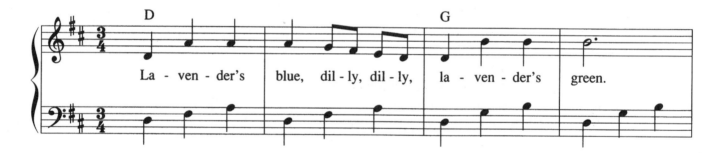

La - ven - der's blue, dil - ly, dil - ly, la - ven - der's green.

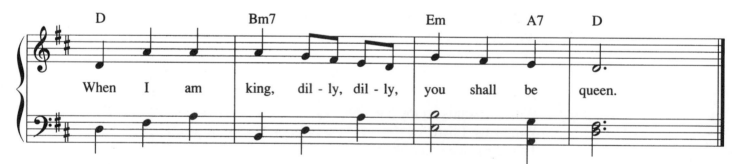

When I am king, dil - ly, dil - ly, you shall be queen.

Verse 2:
Call up your men, dilly dilly,
Set them to work.
Some to the plough, dilly dilly,
Some to the cart.

Verse 3:
Some to make hay, dilly dilly,
Some to make corn.
Whilst you and I, dilly dilly,
Keep ourselves warm.

Verse 4:
Roses are red, dilly dilly,
Violets are blue.
If you love me, dilly dilly,
I will love you.

Verse 5:
Let the birds sing, dilly dilly,
Let the lambs play.
We shall be safe, dilly dilly,
Out of harm's way.

Lazy Katy, Will You Get Up?

Traditional

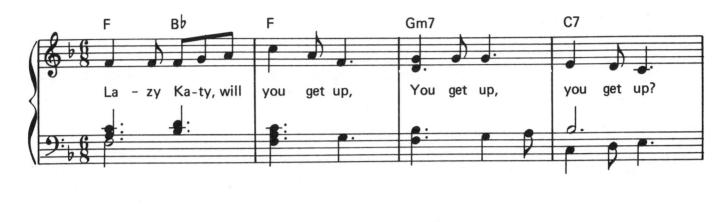

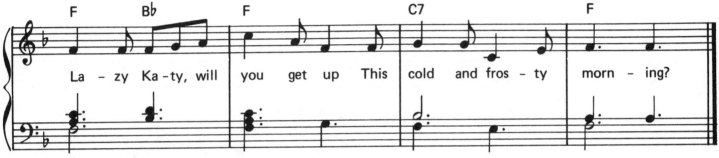

Verse 2:
No mother, I won't get up,
Won't get up, won't get up,
No mother, I won't get up,
This cold and frosty morning.

Verse 3:
What if I give you some bread and jam?
Bread and jam? Bread and jam?
What if I give you some bread and jam?
This cold and frosty morning.

Verse 4:
No mother, I won't get up,
Won't get up, won't get up,
No mother, I won't get up,
This cold and frosty morning.

Verse 5:
What if I give you some bacon and eggs?
Bacon and eggs? Bacon and eggs?
What if I give you some bacon and eggs?
This cold and frosty morning.

Verse 6:
No mother, I won't get up,
Won't get up, won't get up,
No mother, I won't get up,
This cold and frosty morning.

Verse 7:
What if I give you a crack on the head?
Crack on the head? Crack on the head?
What if I give you a crack on the head?
This cold and frosty morning.

Verse 8:
Yes mother, I will get up,
Will get up, will get up,
Yes mother, I will get up,
This cold and frosty morning.

Little Bird, Little Bird

Traditional

Moderately

mf 1. Lit - tle bird, lit - tle bird, go through my win - dow,
(Verse 2 see block lyric)

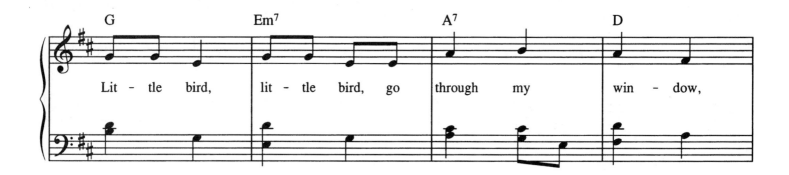

Lit - tle bird, lit - tle bird, go through my win - dow,

Lit - tle bird, lit - tle bird, go through my win - dow, And

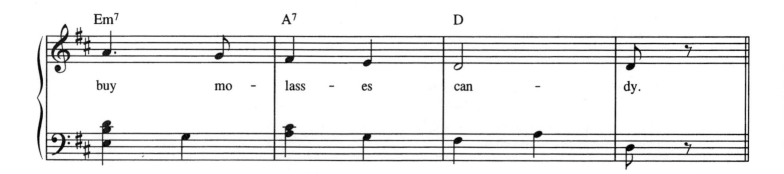

buy mo - lass - es can - dy.

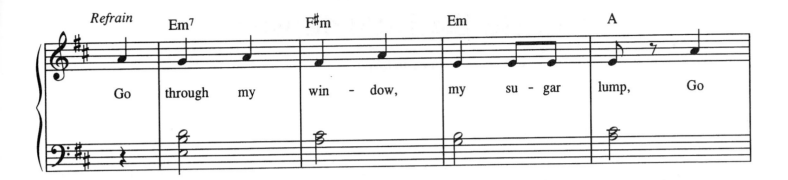

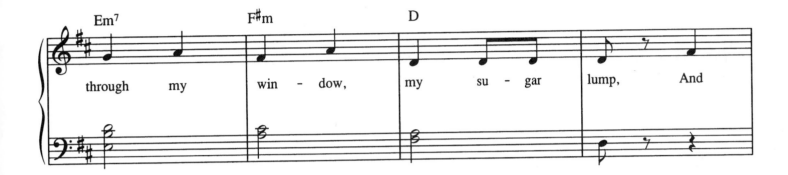

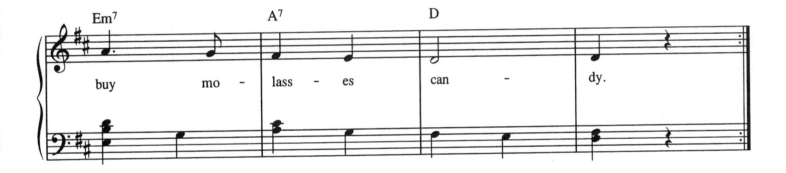

Verse 2:
Blue bird, blue bird,
Fly through my window,
Blue bird, blue bird,
Fly through my window,
Blue bird, blue bird,
Fly through my window,
And buy molasses candy.

Chorus:
Fly through my window,
My little bird,
Fly through my window,
My little bird,
And buy molasses candy.

Little Bo-Peep

Traditional

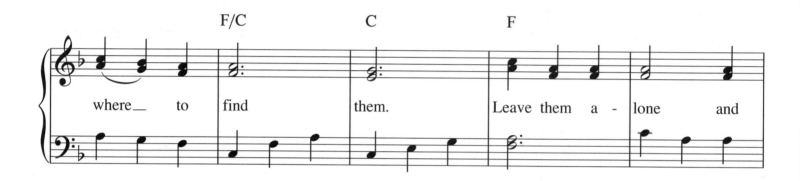

Verse 2:
Little Bo Peep fell fast asleep,
And dreamed she heard them bleating,
But when she awoke, she found it a joke,
For they were still a-fleeting.

Verse 3:
Then up she took her little crook,
Determined for to find them,
She found them indeed, but it made her heart bleed,
For they'd left their tails behind them.

Little Boy Blue

Traditional

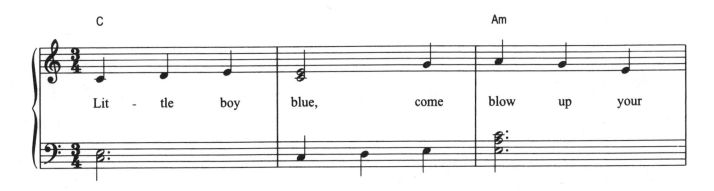

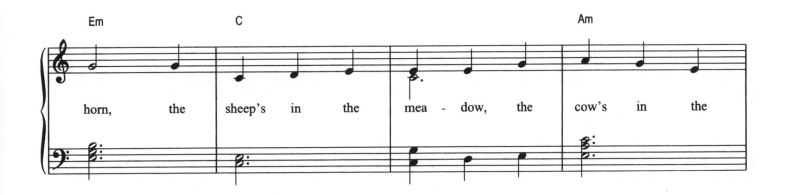

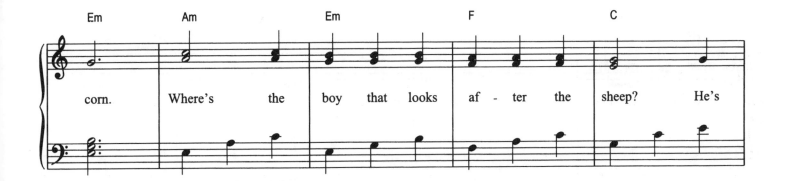

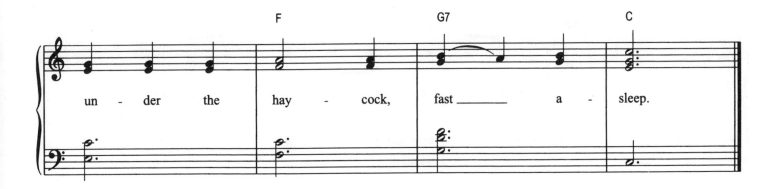

Little Girl

Traditional

Moderately

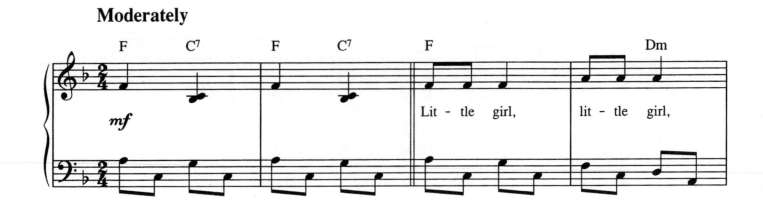

Little Jack Horner

Traditional

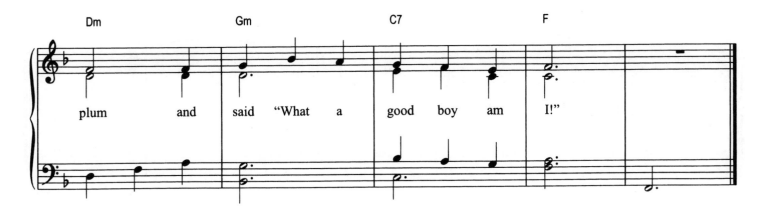

Little Miss Muffet

Traditional

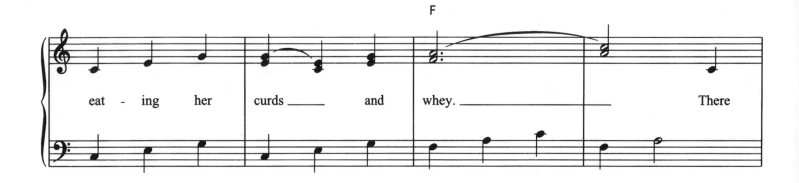

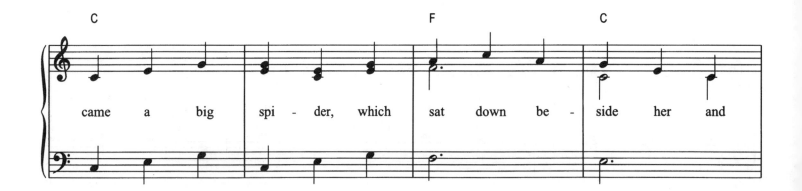

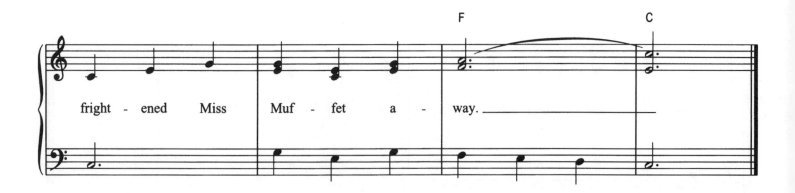

Little Polly Flinders

Traditional

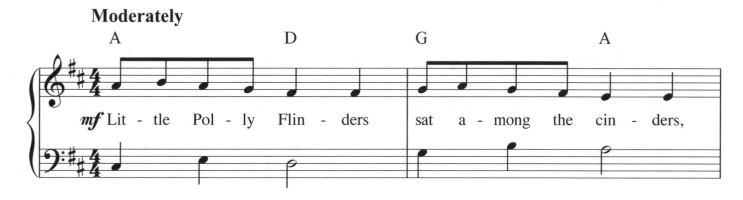

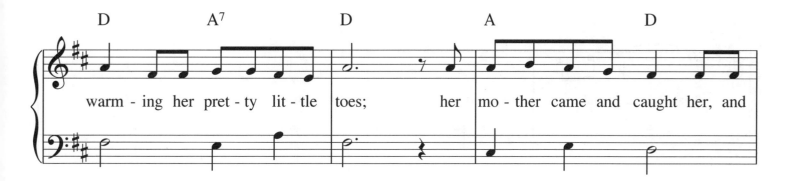

Little Polly Flinders
Sat among the cinders,
Warming her pretty little toes;
Her mother came and caught her,
And smacked her little daughter,
For spoiling her nice new clothes.

Little Tommy Tucker

Traditional

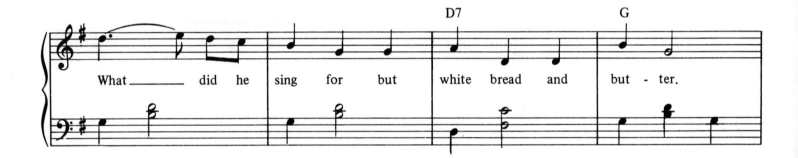

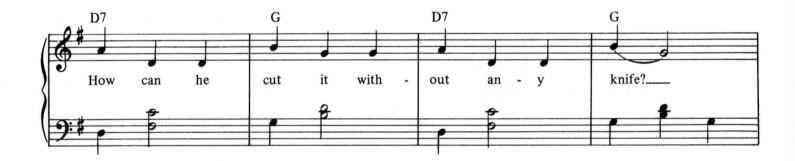

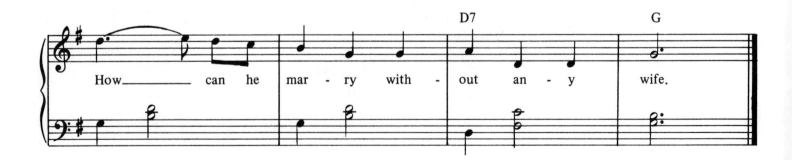

London's Burning

Traditional

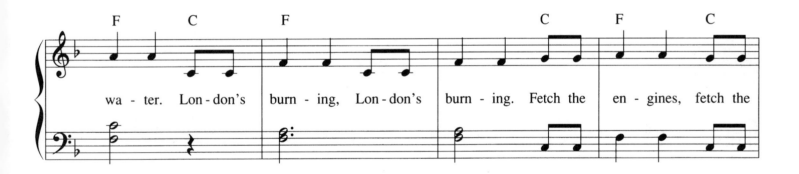

London Bridge Is Falling Down

Traditional

With spirit

1. Lon - don Bridge is fall - ing down, fall - ing down, fall - ing down.

Lon - don Bridge is fall - ing down, my fair la - dy.

Verse 2:
Build it up with iron bars *etc.*

Verse 3:
Iron bars will bend and break *etc.*

Verse 4:
Build it up with pins and needles *etc.*

Verse 5:
Pins and needles rust and bend *etc.*

Verse 6:
Build it up with penny loaves *etc.*

Verse 7:
Penny loaves will tumble down *etc.*

Verse 8:
Build it up with gold and silver *etc.*

Verse 9:
Gold and silver I've not got *etc.*

Verse 10:
Here's a prisoner I have got *etc.*

Verse 11:
What's the prisoner done to you? *etc.*

Verse 12:
Stole my watch and broke my chain *etc.*

Verse 13:
What'll you take to set him free? *etc.*

Verse 14:
One hundred pounds will set him free *etc.*

Verse 15:
One hundred pounds we have not got *etc.*

Verse 16:
Then off to prison he must go *etc.*

Lucy Locket

Traditional

Quickly

Lu - cy Lock - et

Merrily We Roll Along

Traditional

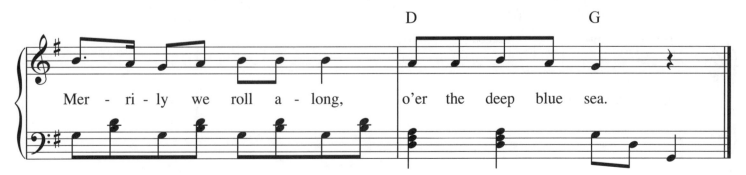

Mary Had A Little Lamb

Traditional

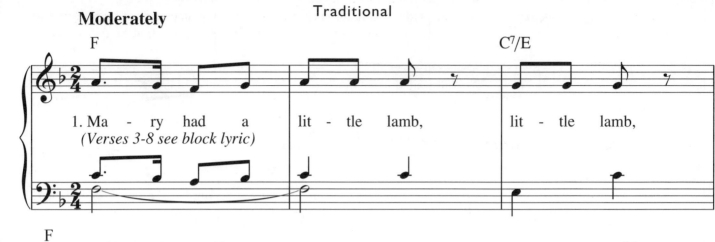

1. Ma - ry had a
(Verses 3-8 see block lyric)
lit - tle lamb, lit - tle lamb,

lit - tle lamb, Ma - ry had a lit - tle lamb, its

fleece as white as snow. 2. And ev - 'ry - where that

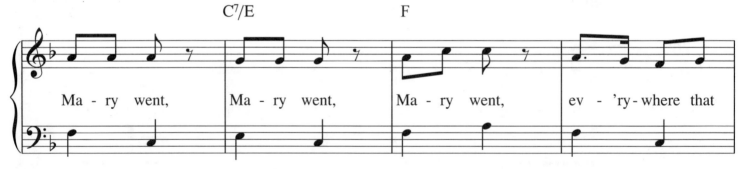

Ma - ry went, Ma - ry went, Ma - ry went, ev - 'ry - where that

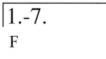

| 1.-7. | 8. |

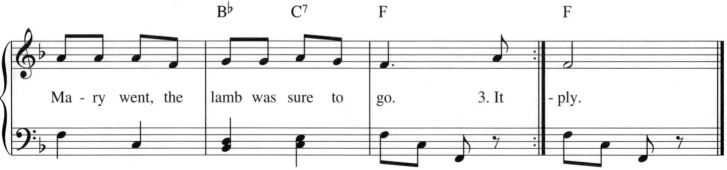

Ma - ry went, the lamb was sure to go. 3. It - ply.

Verse 3:
It followed her to school one day,
School one day, school one day.
It followed her to school one day,
Which was against the rules.

Verse 4:
It made the children laugh and play,
Laugh and play, laugh and play.
It made the children laugh and play,
To see a lamb at school.

Verse 5:
And so the teacher turned it out,
Turned it out, turned it out.
And so the teacher turned it out,
But still it lingered near.

Verse 6:
And waited patiently about,
'Ly about, 'ly about.
And waited patiently about,
'Til Mary did appear.

Verse 7:
Why does the lamb love Mary so?
Mary so, Mary so?
Why does the lamb love Mary so?
The eager children cry.

Verse 8:
Why, Mary loves the lamb, you know,
Lamb, you know, lamb, you know.
Why, Mary loves the lamb, you know,
The teacher did reply.

Mary, Mary, Quite Contrary

Traditional

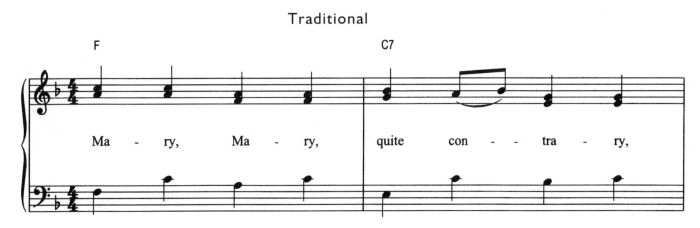

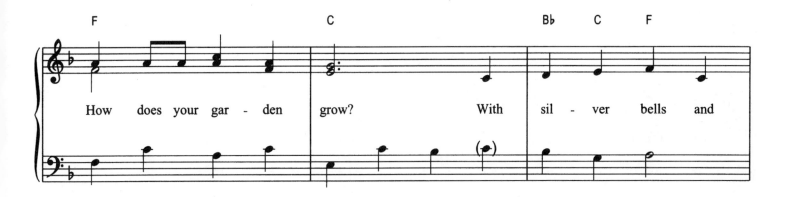

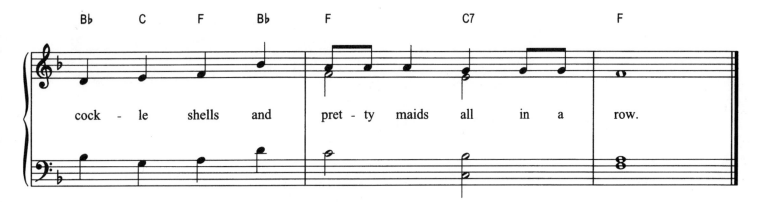

Michael Finnegan

Traditional

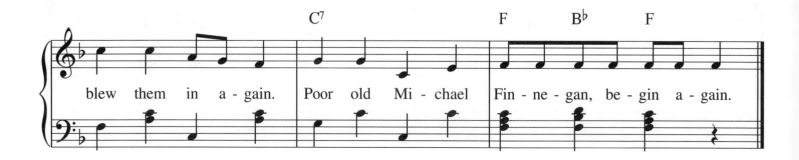

Verse 2:
There was an old man called Michael Finnegan,
He went fishing with a pin again.
He caught a fish then dropped it in again.
Poor old Michael Finnegan, begin again.

Michael Row The Boat Ashore

Traditional

Moderately

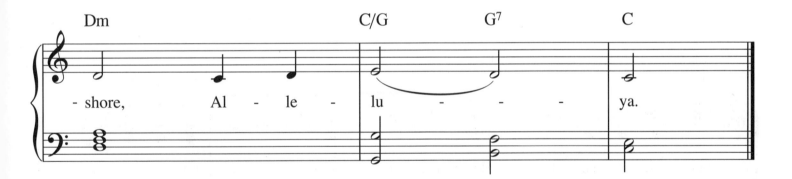

Verse 2:
Sister, help to trim the sail,
Alleluya,
Sister, help to trim the sail,
Alleluya.

Verse 3:
Michael's boat is a gospel boat,
Alleluya,
Michael's boat is a gospel boat,
Alleluya.

Verse 4:
Jordan's river is chilly and cold,
Alleluya,
Jordan's river is chilly and cold,
Alleluya.

Verse 5:
Jordan's river is deep and wide,
Alleluya,
Jordan's river is deep and wide,
Alleluya.

Miss Polly Had A Dolly

Traditional

Moderately

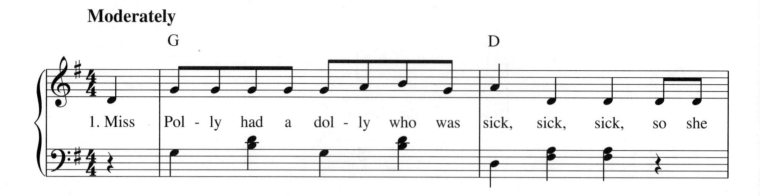

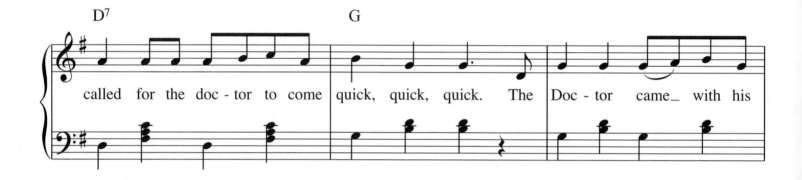

Verse 2:
He looked at the dolly and he shook his head,
He said, "Miss Polly, put her straight to bed".
He wrote on the paper for a pill, pill, pill,
"I'll be back the morning with my bill, bill, bill."

My Hat It Has Three Corners

Traditional

Moderately

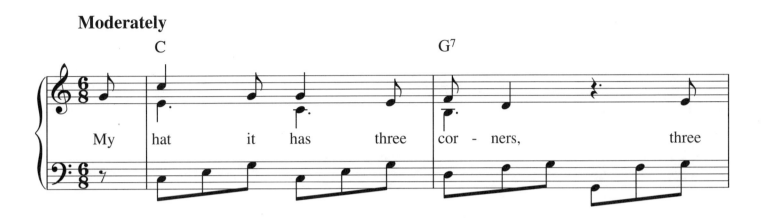

My hat it has three cor - ners, three

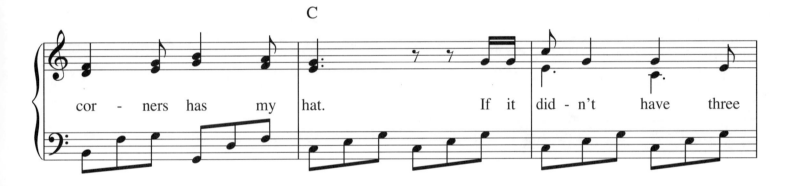

cor - ners has my hat. If it did - n't have three

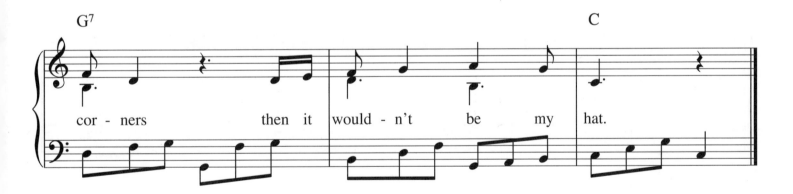

cor - ners then it would - n't be my hat.

My hat it has three corners,
Three corners has my hat.
If it didn't have three corners
Then it wouldn't be my hat.

My Lady's Garden

Traditional

Moderately

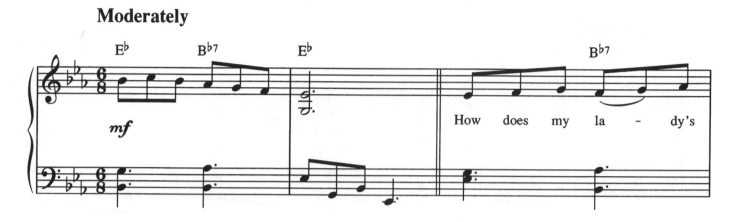

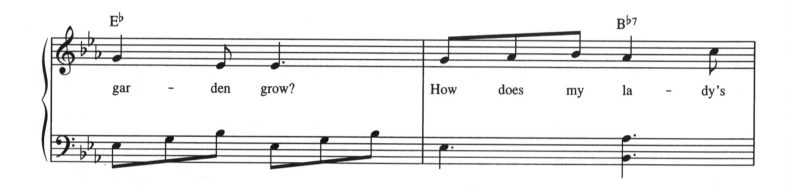

How does my la-dy's gar-den grow? How does my la-dy's

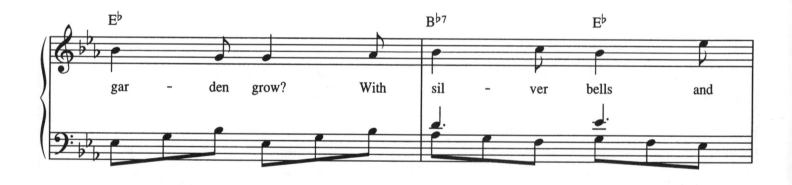

gar-den grow? With sil-ver bells and

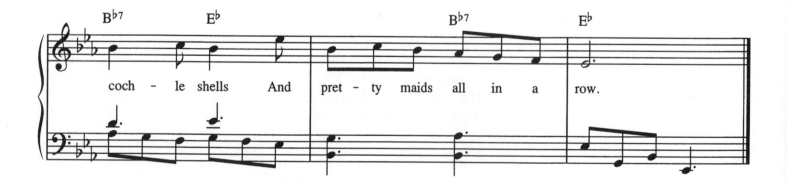

coch-le shells And pret-ty maids all in a row.

Nobody Loves Me

Traditional

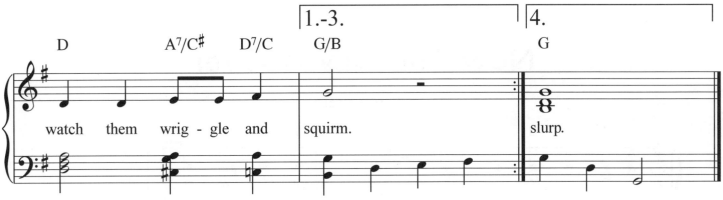

Verse 2:
Bite their heads off, suck their juice out,
Throw their skins away.
I don't see how birds can live on
Worms three times a day.

Verse 3:
Nobody loves me, everybody hates me,
Going to the garden to eat worms.
Long thin slimy ones, short fat juicy ones,
Gooey, gooey, gooey, gooey worms.

Verse 4:
Long thin slimy ones slip down easily,
Short fat juicy ones stick,
Short fat juicy ones stick between your teeth
And the juice goes slurp, slurp, slurp.

Now I Lay Me Down To Sleep

Traditional

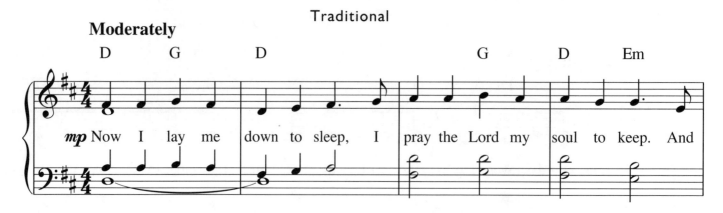

Now I lay me down to sleep, I pray the Lord my soul to keep. And

if I die be - fore I wake, I pray the Lord my soul to take.

Now The Day Is Over

Traditional

Now the day is o - ver night is draw-ing nigh,

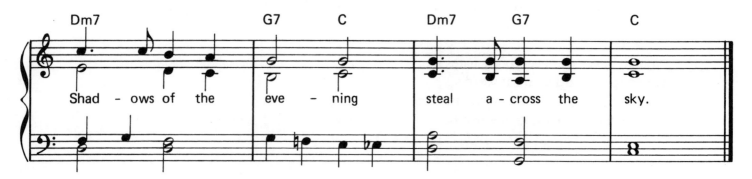

Shad - ows of the eve - ning steal a - cross the sky.

Oh, We Can Play On The Big Bass Drum

Traditional

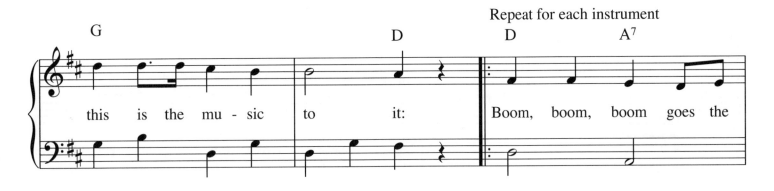

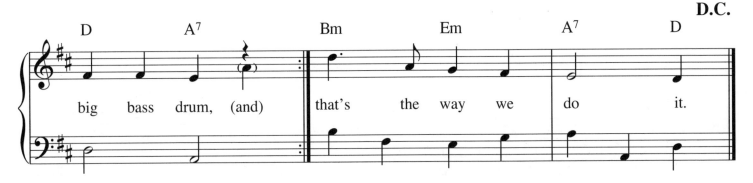

Verse 2:
Oh, we can play on the tambourine,
And this is the music to it:
Chink, chink, chink goes the tambourine,
Boom, boom, boom goes the big bass drum,
And that's the way we do it.

Verse 3:
Oh, we can play on the castanets,
And this is the music to it:
Click, clickety-click go the castanets,
Chink, chink, chink goes the tambourine, *etc.*

Verse 4:
Oh, we can play on the triangle,
And this is the music to it:
Ping, ping, ping goes the triangle,
Click, clickety-click go the castanets, *etc.*

Verse 5:
Oh, we can play on the old banjo,
And this is the music to it:
Tum, tum, tum goes the old banjo,
Ping, ping, ping goes the triangle, *etc.*

Oh Dear!
What Can The Matter Be?

Traditional

Moderately quick

What can the mat - ter be? Oh dear! What can the mat - ter be?

Oh dear! What can the mat - ter be? John - ny's so long at the

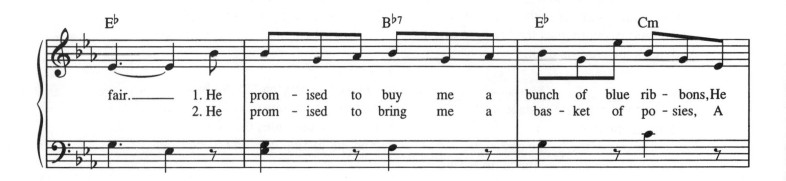

fair._____ 1. He prom - ised to buy me a bunch of blue rib - bons, He
2. He prom - ised to bring me a bas - ket of po - sies, A

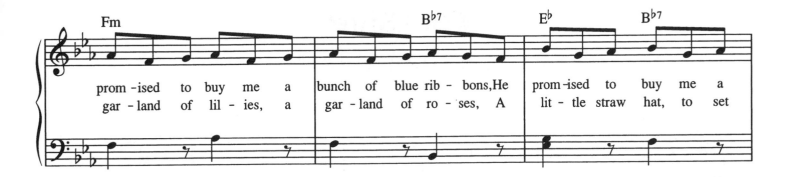

Fm ... Bb7 Eb Bb7

prom -ised to buy me a | bunch of blue rib - bons,He | prom -ised to buy me a
gar - land of lil - ies, a | gar - land of ro - ses, A | lit - tle straw hat, to set

Eb Cm Fm7 Bb7 **1.** Eb

bunch of blue rib - bons To | tie up my bon - ny brown | hair._____ And it's
off the blue rib - bons That | tie up my bon - ny brown

2. Eb Eb

hair._____ And it's | Oh dear! | What can the mat - ter be?

Fm Bb7 Eb

Oh dear! | What can the mat - ter be? | Oh dear!

Fm Bb7 Eb

What can the mat - ter be? | John -ny's so long at the | fair.

Old Blue

Traditional

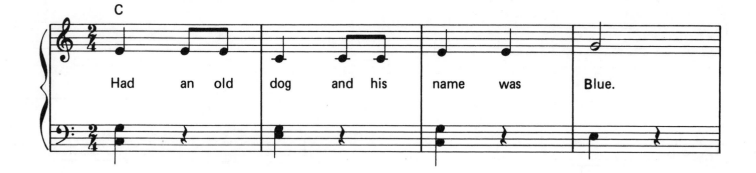

Had an old dog and his name was Blue.

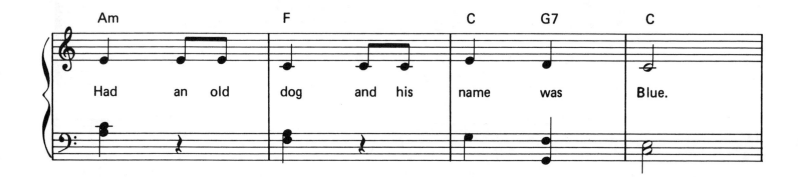

Had an old dog and his name was Blue.

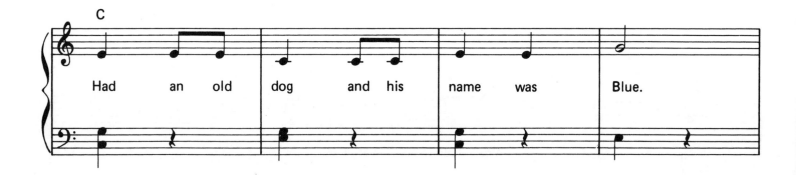

Had an old dog and his name was Blue.

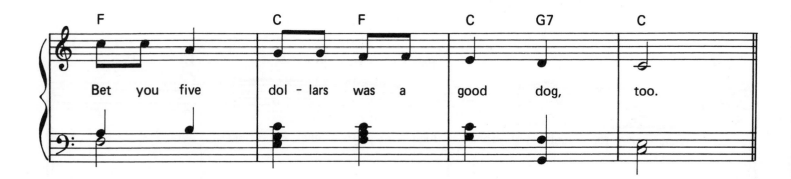

Bet you five dol-lars was a good dog, too.

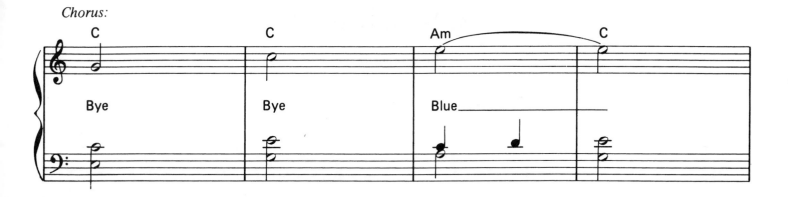

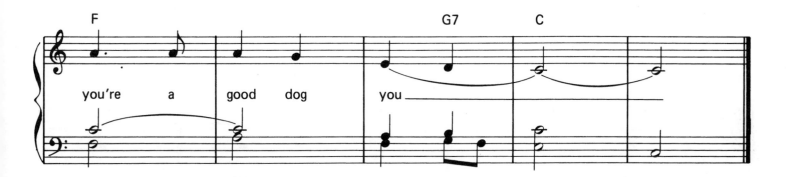

Chorus:
Bye bye Blue
You're a good dog you.

Verse 2:
Every night just about dark (3 times)
Blue goes out and begins to bark.

Bye bye Blue *etc.*

Verse 3:
Everything just in a rush (3 times)
He treed a possum in a white-oak bush.

Bye bye Blue *etc.*

Verse 4:
Possum walked out to the end of a limb (3 times)
Blue set down and talked to him.

Bye bye Blue *etc.*

Verse 5:
Blue got sick and very sick (3 times)
Sent for the doctor to come here quick.

Bye bye Blue *etc.*

Verse 6:
Doctor come and he come in a run (3 times)
Says, "Old Blue, your hunting's done".

Bye bye Blue *etc.*

Verse 7:
Blue he died and died so hard (3 times)
Scratched little holes all around the yard.

Bye bye Blue *etc.*

Verse 8:
Laid him out in a shady place (3 times)
Covered him o'er with a possum's face.

Bye bye Blue *etc.*

Verse 9:
When I get to heaven I'll tell you what I'll do
(3 times)
I'll take my horn and blow for Blue.

Bye bye Blue *etc.*

Old Davey Jones

Traditional

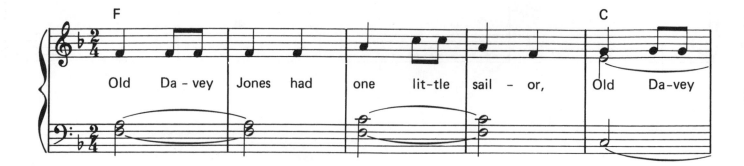

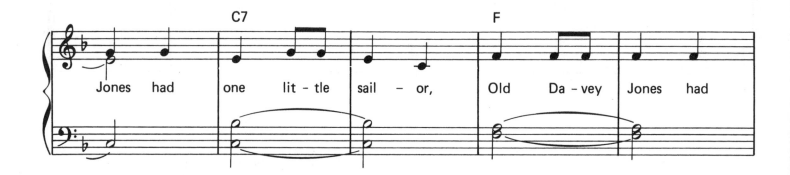

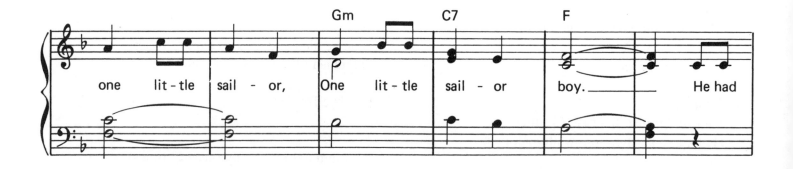

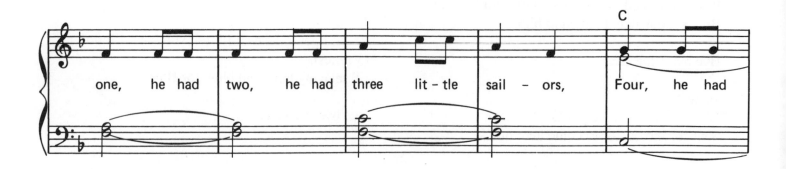

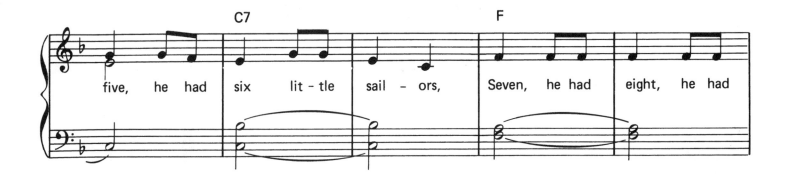

five, he had six lit - tle sail - ors, Seven, he had eight, he had

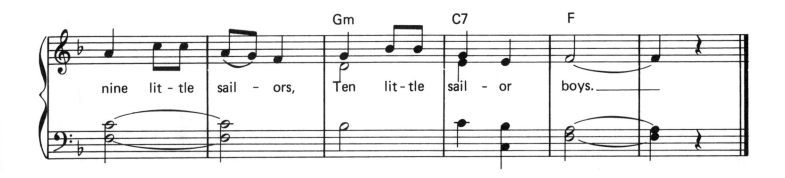

nine lit - tle sail - ors, Ten lit - tle sail - or boys.

Chorus:
Old Davey Jones had ten little sailors *etc.*

Verse 2:
He had ten, he had nine, he had eight little sailors,
Seven, he had six, he had five little sailors,
Four, he had three, he had two little sailors,
One little sailor boy.

Old Hogan's Goat

Traditional

Moderately

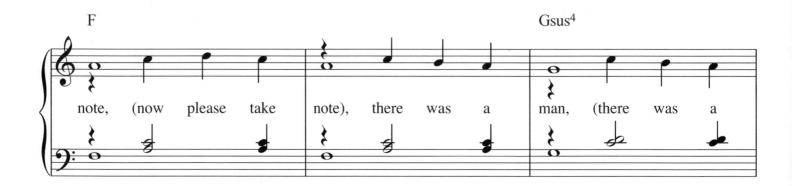

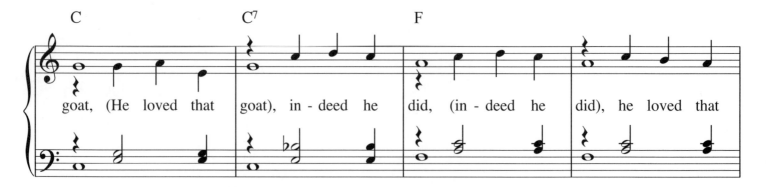

goat, (he loved that goat), just like a kid, (just like a kid).

Verse 2:

One day that goat	(one day that goat)
Was feeling fine	(was feeling fine)
Ate three red shirts	(ate three red shirts)
From off the line	(from off the line)
The old man grabbed	(the old man grabbed)
Her by the back	(her by the back)
And tied her to	(and tied her to)
The railway track	(the railway track)

Verse 3:

Now when the train	(now when the train)
Came into sight	(came into sight)
The goat grew pale	(the goat grew pale)
And grey with fright	(and grey with fright)
She struggled hard	(she struggled hard)
And then again	(and then again)
Coughed up the shirts	(coughed up the shirts)
And flagged the train	(and flagged the train)

Old King Cole

Traditional

Old King Cole was a mer-ry old __ soul and a mer-ry old soul was he; He __

called for his pipe, and he called for his bowl, And he called for his fid - dlers __ three.

Ev - 'ry __ fid-dler had a fid-dle so __ fine, and a ve - ry fine __ fid-dle had he. Oh there's

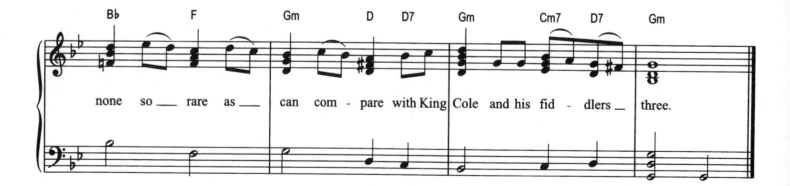

none so __ rare as __ can com - pare with King Cole and his fid - dlers __ three.

Old MacDonald Had A Farm

Traditional

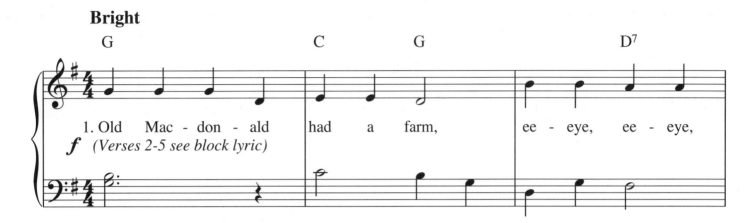

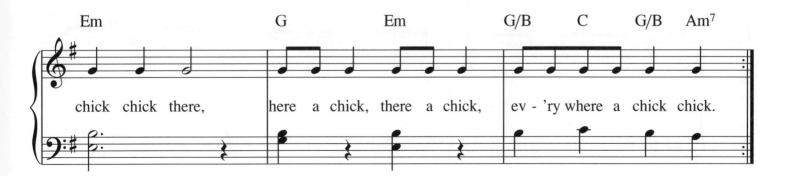

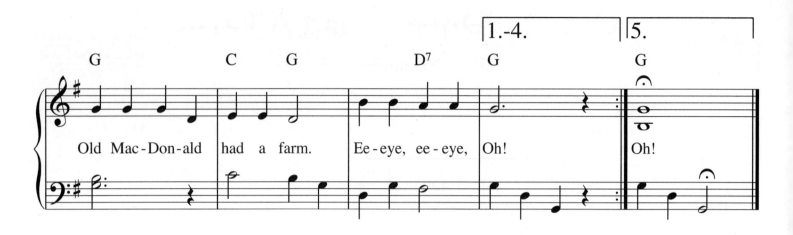

Verse 2:
Old MacDonald had a farm,
Ee-eye, ee-eye, oh!
And on that farm he had some ducks,
Ee-eye, ee-eye, oh!
With a quack-quack here and a quack-quack there,
Here a quack, there a quack, everywhere a quack-quack.
Chick-chick here and a chick-chick there,
Here a chick, there a chick, everywhere a chick-chick.
Old MacDonald had a farm,
Ee-eye, ee-eye, oh!

Verse 3:
…and on that farm he had some cows…
With a moo-moo here and a moo-moo there,
Here a moo, there a moo, everywhere a moo-moo,
Quack-quack here and a quack-quack there…
Chick-chick here and a chick-chick there…

Verse 4:
…and on that farm he had some pigs…
With an oink-oink here and an oink-oink there,
Here an oink, there an oink, everywhere an oink-oink,
Moo-moo here…
Quack-quack here…
Chick-chick here…

Verse 5:
…and on that farm he had some sheep…
With a baa-baa here and a baa-baa there…
Oink-oink here…
Moo-moo here…
Quack-quack here…
Chick-chick here…

Old Mother Hubbard

Traditional

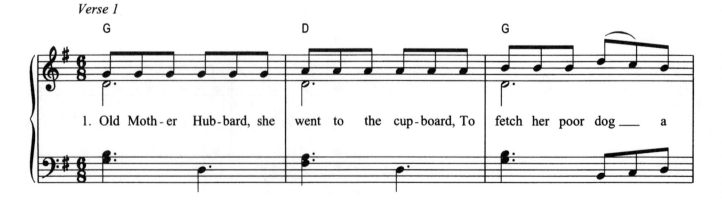

bone _____   When she got there, the   cup - board was bare,   And

so the poor dog ___ had none.   *Verses 2 - 14*   2. She went to the ba - ker's to

buy him some bread, But   when she came back the   poor dog was dead.

Verse 3:
She went to the undertaker's
To buy him a coffin:
But when she came back,
The poor dog was laughing.

Verse 4:
She took a clean dish
To get him some tripe:
But when she got back,
He was smoking a pipe.

Verse 5:
She went to the fishmonger's
To buy him some fish:
But when she came back,
He was licking the dish.

Verse 6:
She went to the tavern
For white wine and red:
But when she got back,
The dog stood on his head.

Verse 7:
She went to the fruiterer's
To buy him some fruit:
But when she came back,
He was playing the flute.

Verse 8:
She went to the tailor's
To buy him a coat:
But when she came back,
He was riding a goat.

Verse 9:
She went to the hatter's
To buy him a hat:
But when she came back,
He was feeding the cat.

Verse 10:
She went to the barber's
To buy him a wig:
But when she came back,
He was dancing a jig.

Verse 11:
She went to the cobbler's
To buy him some shoes:
But when she came back,
He was reading the news.

Verse 12:
She went to the seamstress
To buy him some linen:
But when she came back,
The dog was a-spinning.

Verse 13:
She went to the hosier's
To buy him some hose:
But when she came back,
He was dressed in his clothes.

Verse 14:
The Dame made a curtsey,
The dog made a bow;
The Dame said, "your servant",
The dog said, "bow-wow".

Oh Where, Oh Where
Has My Little Dog Gone?

Words by Septimus Winner

One Elephant

Traditional

One* elephant went out to play
Upon a spider's web one day.
He found it such enormous fun
That he called for another elephant to come.

* amend number accordingly

Activity:
Get everyone into a circle. Pick one person to be the elephant and ask them to stand in the middle. While singing, the elephant in the middle skips around having fun. Those on the outside can mime appropriate actions to match the song. On the line 'that he called for another elephant to come', everyone wiggles their bottom and the elephant in the middle points at someone to come and join him/her. Keep going until everyone is an elephant!

One Finger, One Thumb

Traditional

Fairly fast

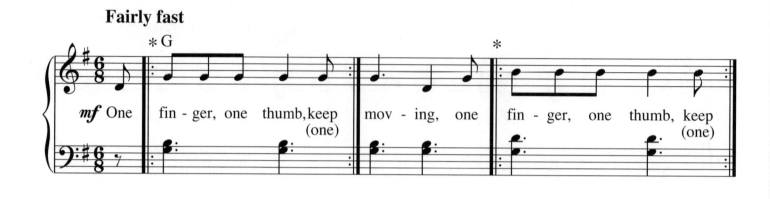

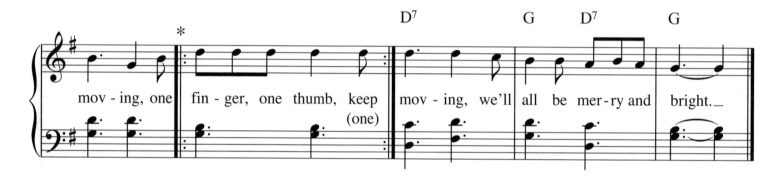

*Repeat as needed in verses 2 to 6

Verse 2:
One finger, one thumb, one arm,
keep moving, *etc.*

Verse 3:
One finger, one thumb, one arm, one leg,
keep moving, *etc.*

Verse 4:
One finger, one thumb, one arm, one leg,
One nod of the head, keep moving, *etc.*

Verse 5:
One finger, one thumb, one arm, one leg,
One nod of the head, stand up, sit down,
keep moving, *etc.*

Verse 6:
One finger, one thumb, one arm, one leg,
One nod of the head, stand up, sit down,
Turn around, keep moving, *etc.*

One Man Went To Mow

Traditional

Fast

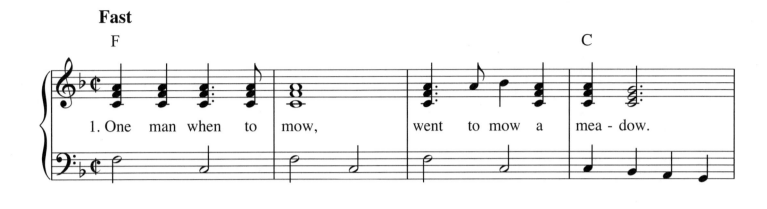

1. One man when to mow, went to mow a mea-dow.

Repeat as required   D.C. **Final bar**

One man and his dog went to mow a mea-dow.

Verse 2:
Two men went to mow,
Went to mow a meadow.
Two men, one man and his dog
Went to mow a meadow.

Verse 3:
Three men went to mow,
Went to mow a meadow.
Three men, two men, one man and his dog
Went to mow a meadow.

Verse 4:
Four men went to mow, *etc.*

Verse 5:
Five men went to mow, *etc.*

Verse 6:
Six men went to mow, *etc.*

Verse 7:
Seven men went mow, *etc.*

One, Two, Buckle My Shoe

Traditional

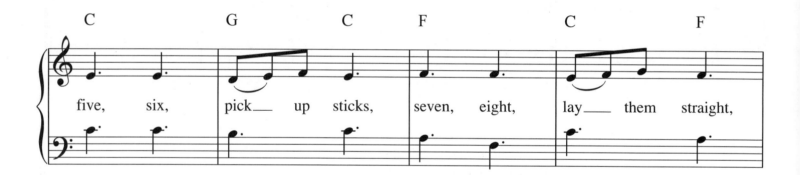

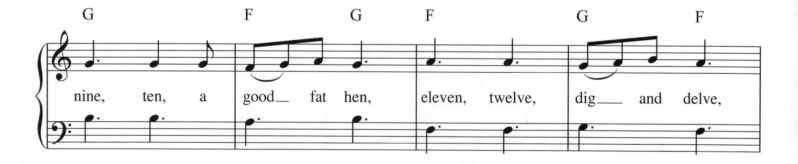

Thir - teen, four - teen, maids___ a - court - ing, fif - teen, six - teen,

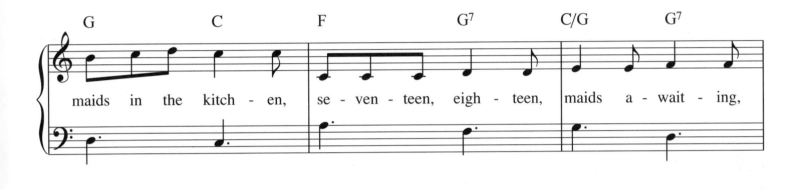

maids in the kitch - en, se - ven - teen, eigh - teen, maids a - wait - ing,

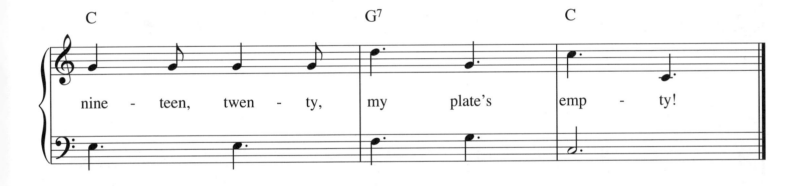

nine - teen, twen - ty, my plate's emp - ty!

One, two, buckle my shoe,
Three, four, open the door,
Five, six, pick up sticks,
Seven, eight, lay them straight,
Nine, ten, a good fat hen,
Eleven, twelve, dig and delve,
Thirteen, fourteen, maids a-courting,
Fifteen, sixteen, maids in the kitchen,
Seventeen, eighteen, maids a-waiting,
Nineteen, twenty, my plate's empty!

On Top Of Old Smoky

Traditional

Moderately

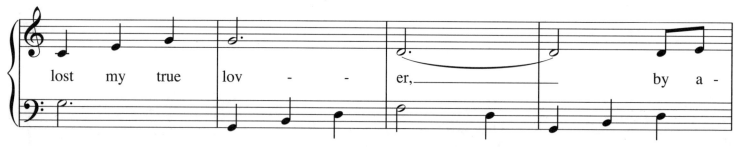

Verse 2:
Well a-courting's a pleasure,
And parting is grief.
But a false-hearted lover
Is worse than a thief.

Verse 3:
A thief he will rob you
And take all you have,
But a false-hearted lover
Will send you to your grave.

Verse 4:
And the grave will decay you
And turn you to dust.
And where is the young man
A poor girl can trust?

Verse 5:
They'll hug you and kiss you
And tell you more lies
Than the cross-ties on the railroad,
Or the stars in the skies.

Verse 6:
They'll tell you they love you
Just to give your heart ease.
But the minute your back's turned,
They'll court whom they please.

One, Two, Three, Four, Five

Traditional

One two, three, four, five, once I caught a fish a - live.

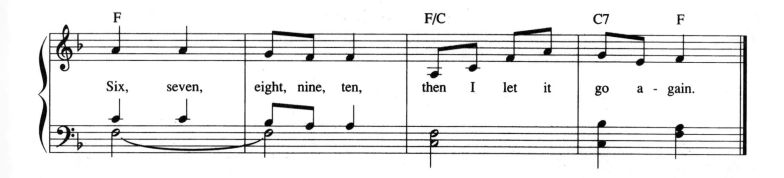

Six, seven, eight, nine, ten, then I let it go a - gain.

Verse 2:
Why did you let it go?
Because it bit my finger so.
Which finger did it bite?
This little finger on the right.

Oranges And Lemons

Traditional

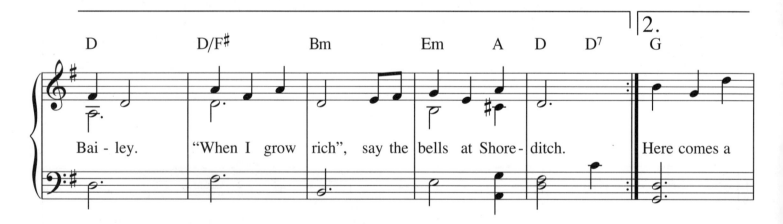

Pat-A-Cake, Pat-A-Cake, Baker's Man

Traditional

Moderately

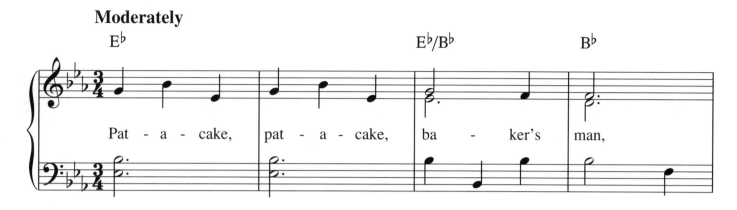

Pat - a - cake, pat - a - cake, ba - ker's man,

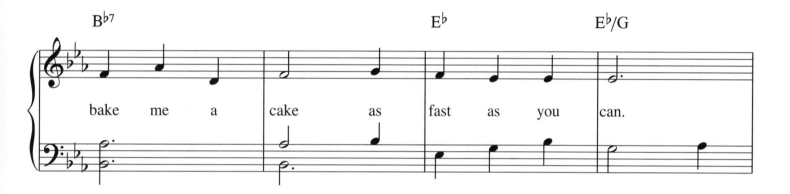

bake me a cake as fast as you can.

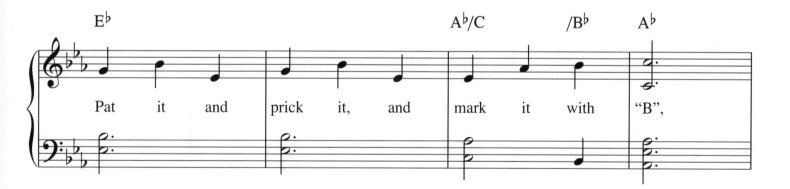

Pat it and prick it, and mark it with "B",

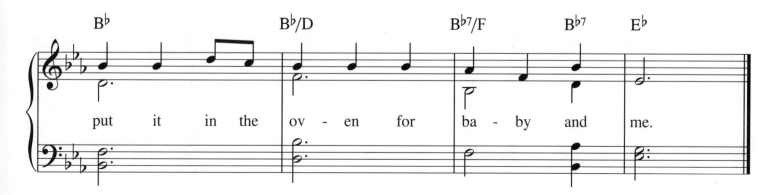

put it in the ov - en for ba - by and me.

Peanut Sat On A Railroad Track

Traditional

Moderately

pea - nut sat on a rail - road track; his heart was all a - flut - ter. A-

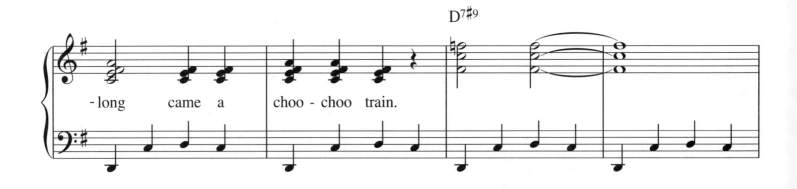

-long came a choo - choo train.

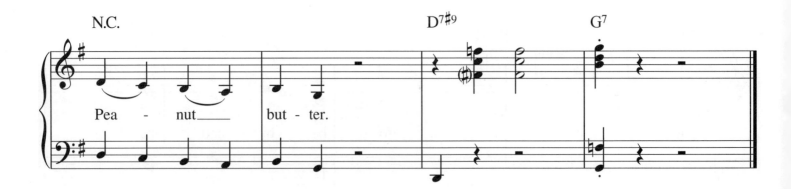

Pea - nut___ but - ter.

Pease Porridge Hot

Traditional

Pease por-ridge hot, Pease por-ridge cold, Pease por-ridge in the pot nine days old.

Peter, Peter, Pumpkin Eater

Traditional

Quickly

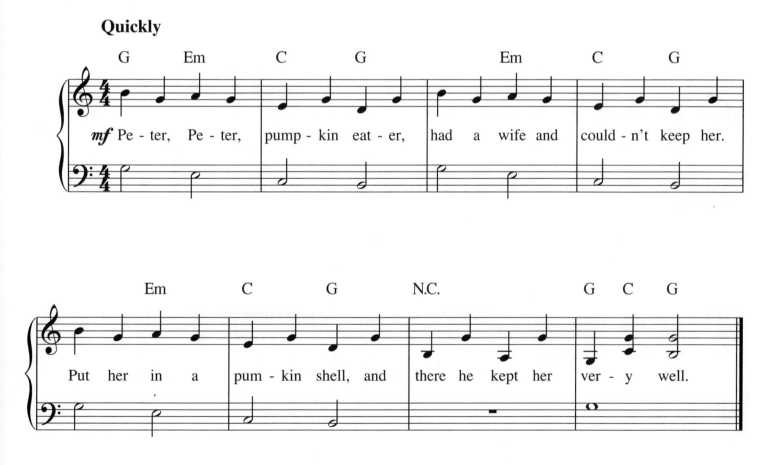

Pe - ter, Pe - ter, pump - kin eat - er, had a wife and could - n't keep her.

Put her in a pum - kin shell, and there he kept her ver - y well.

Peter Piper

Traditional

Fairly fast

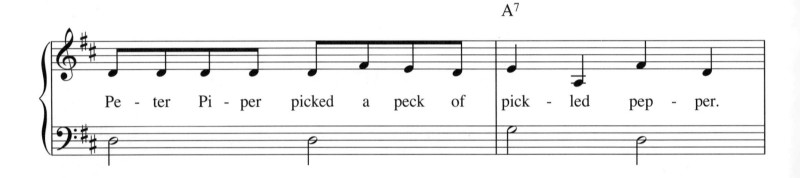

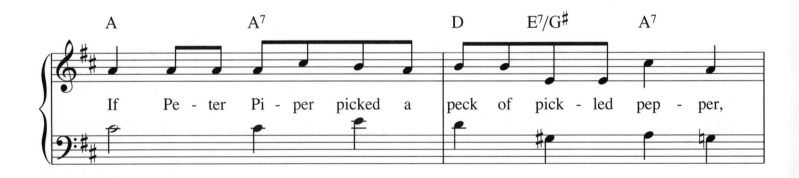

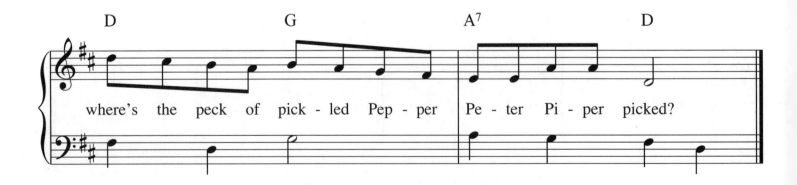

Polly Put The Kettle On

Traditional

Moderately

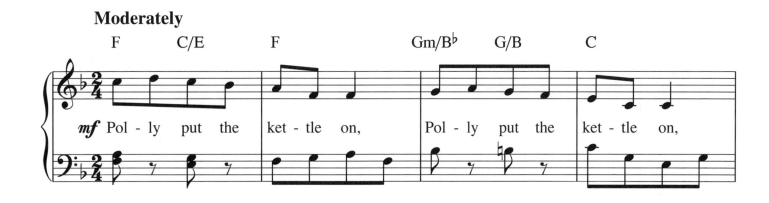

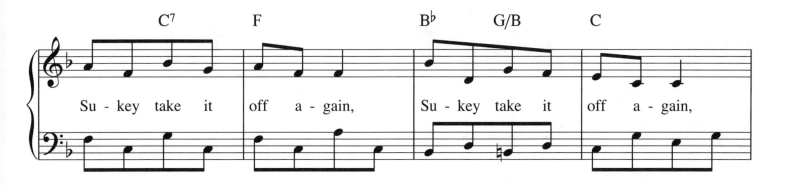

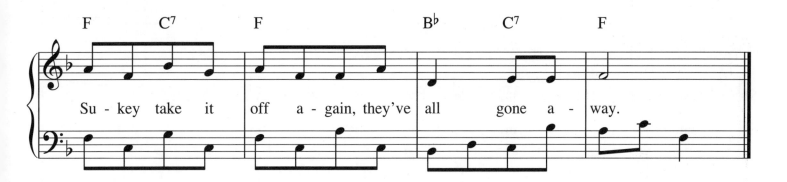

Polly Wolly Doodle

Traditional

Bright, with humour

mp

1. Oh, I

went down South for to see my Sal, sing - ing Pol - ly Wol - ly Doo - dle all the

day. My___ Sal she is a spunk - y gal, sing - ing

Pol - ly Wol - ly Doo - dle all the day. Fare thee well, fare thee

well. Fare thee well, my fair - y fay. For I'm

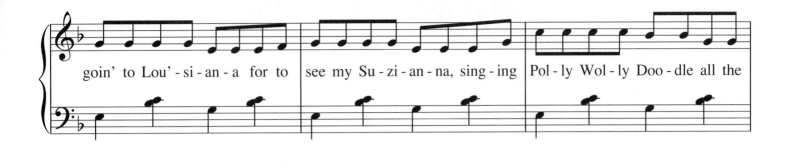

goin' to Lou'-si-an-a for to see my Su-zi-an-na, sing-ing Pol-ly Wol-ly Doo-dle all the

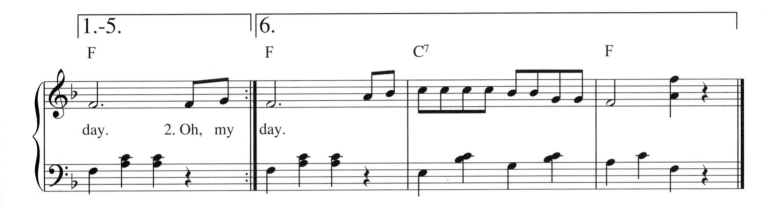

1.-5. F

day.   2. Oh, my day.

6. F   C⁷   F

Chorus:
Fare thee well, fare thee well.
Fare thee well, my fairy fay.
For I'm goin' to Lou'siana for to see my Suzianna,
Singing Polly Wolly Doodle all the day.

Verse 2:
Oh, my Sal she is a maiden fair,
Singing Polly Wolly Doodle all the day.
With laughing eyes and curly hair,
Singing Polly Wolly Doodle all the day.

Fare thee well, fare thee well. *etc.*

Verse 3:
Oh, a grasshopper sittin' on a railroad track,
Singing Polly Wolly Doodle all the day.
A pickin' his teeth with a carpet tack,
Singing Polly Wolly Doodle all the day.

Fare thee well, fare thee well. *etc.*

Verse 4:
Oh, I went to bed, but it wasn't no use,
Singing Polly Wolly Doodle all the day.
My feet stuck out like a chicken roost,
Singing Polly Wolly Doodle all the day.

Fare thee well, fare thee well. *etc.*

Verse 5:
Behind the barn, down on my knees,
Singing Polly Wolly Doodle all the day.
I thought I heard a chicken sneeze,
Singing Polly Wolly Doodle all the day.

Fare thee well, fare thee well. *etc.*

Verse 6:
He sneezed so hard with the whooping cough,
Singing Polly Wolly Doodle all the day.
He sneezed his head and tail right off,
Singing Polly Wolly Doodle all the day.

Fare thee well, fare thee well. *etc.*

Pop Goes The Weasel

Traditional

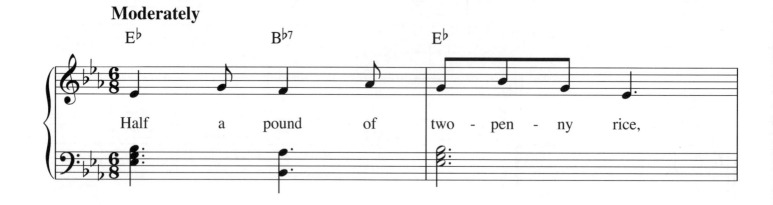

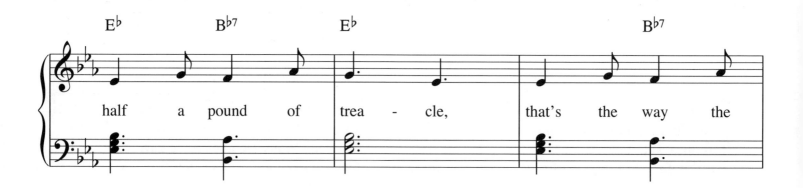

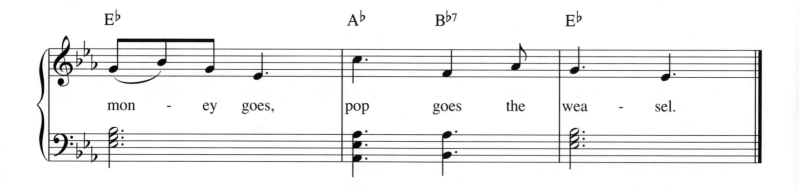

Half a pound of two-penny rice,
Half a pound of treacle,
That's the way the money goes,
Pop goes the weasel.

Pussy Cat, Pussy Cat

Traditional

Cheerfully

"Pus - sy cat, pus - sy cat,

where have you been?" "I've been_____ to Lon - don to

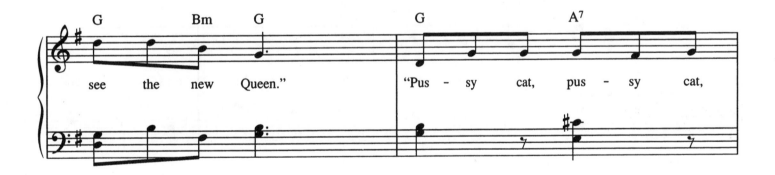

see the new Queen." "Pus - sy cat, pus - sy cat,

what did you there?" "I caught___ a lit - tle mouse un - der her chair."

Ride A Cock Horse

Traditional

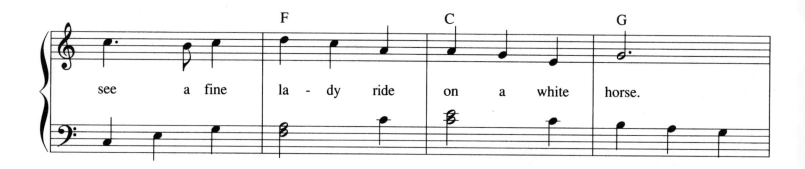

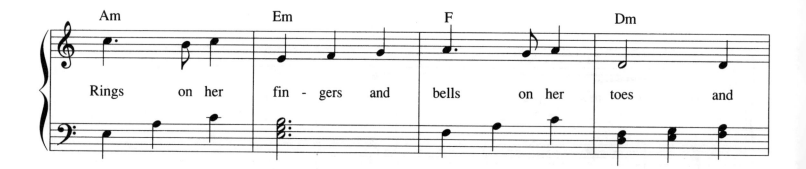

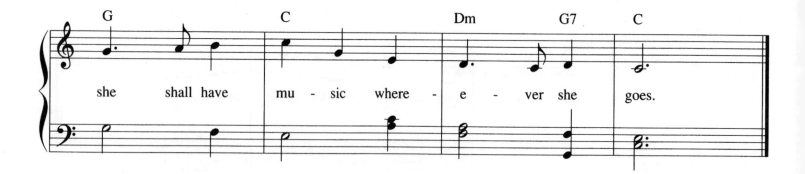

Ring-A-Ring O' Roses

Traditional

Moderately

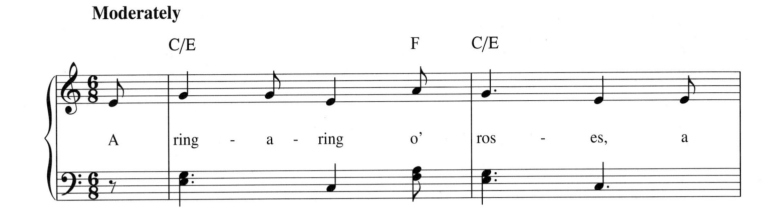

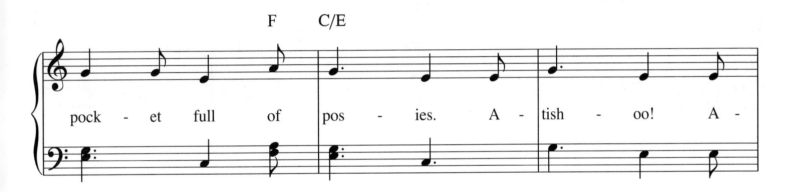

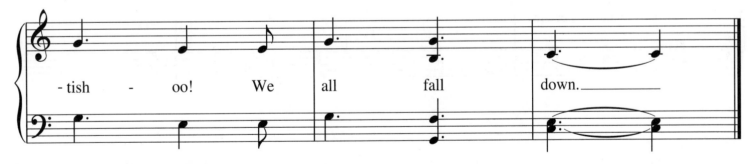

A ring a ring o' roses,
A pocket full of posies.
Atishoo! Atishoo!
We all fall down.

Rock-A-Bye Baby

Traditional

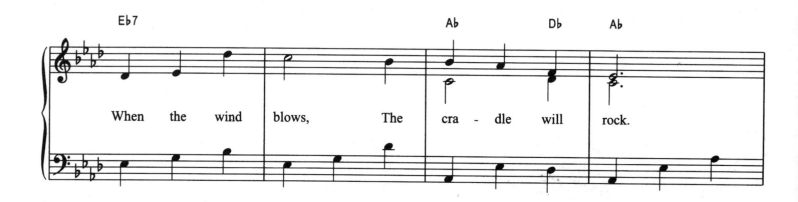

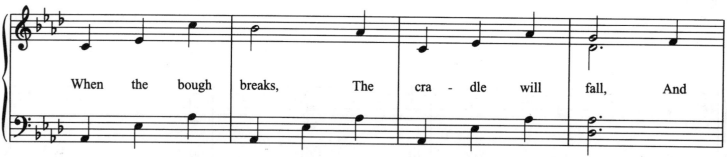

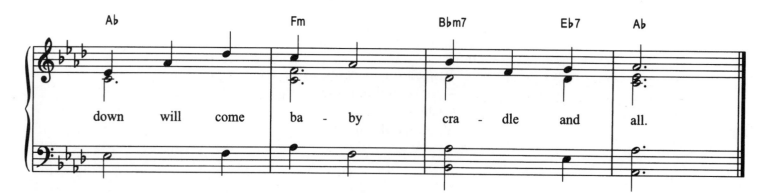

Round The Village

Traditional

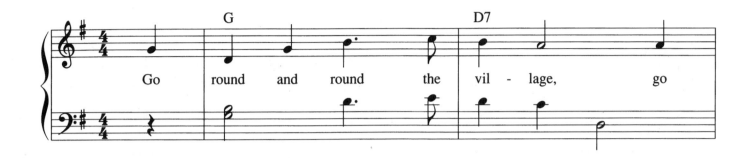

Go round and round the vil - lage, go

round and round the vil - lage. Go round and round the

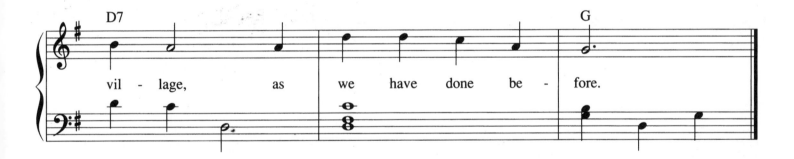

vil - lage, as we have done be - fore.

Verse 2:
Go in and out the windows,
Go in and out the windows,
Go in and out the windows,
As we have done before.

Verse 3:
Now stand and face your partner,
Now stand and face your partner,
Now stand and face your partner,
And bow before you go.

Verse 4:
Now follow me to London,
Now follow me to London,
Now follow me to London,
As we have done before.

Verse 5:
Now shake his hand and leave him,
Now shake his hand and leave him,
Now shake his hand and leave him,
And bow before you go.

Row, Row, Row Your Boat

Traditional

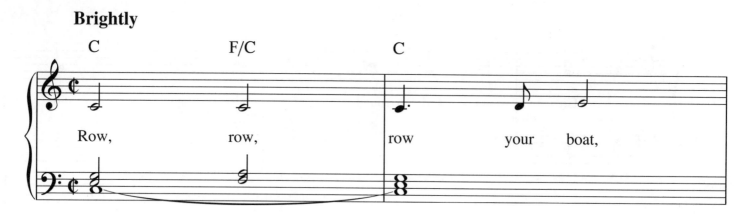

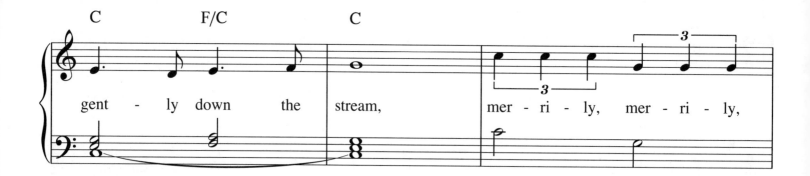

Row, row, row your boat,
Gently down the stream,
Merrily, merrily, merrily, merrily,
Life is but a dream.

Rub-A-Dub-Dub,
Three Men In A Tub

Traditional

Moderately

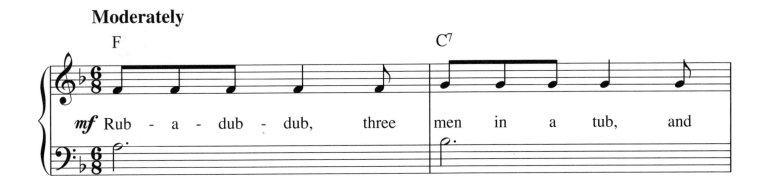

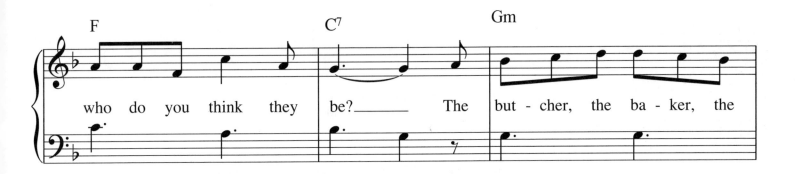

Rub-a-dub-dub, three men in a tub,
And who do you think they be?
The butcher, the baker, the candlestick maker,
So turn out the knaves, all three.

Round And Round The Garden

Traditional

Round and round the gar - den like a ted - dy bear.

One step, two step and tick - le - y un - der there!

See-Saw, Margery Daw

Traditional

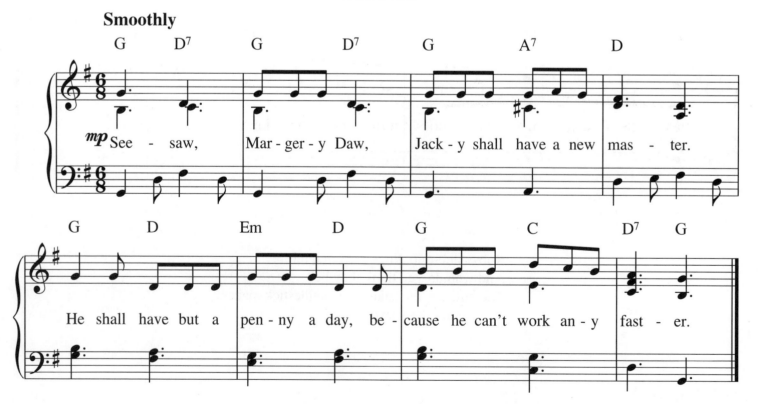

See - saw, Mar - ger - y Daw, Jack - y shall have a new mas - ter.

He shall have but a pen - ny a day, be - cause he can't work an - y fast - er.

Simple Simon

Traditional

Verse 2:
Said the pieman unto Simon,
"Show me first your penny."
Said Simple Simon to the pieman,
"Indeed I have not any."

Verse 3:
Simple Simon went a-fishing,
For to catch a whale;
But all the water he had got
Was in his mother's pail.

Verse 4:
Simple Simon went to look,
If plums grew on a thistle;
He pricked his fingers very much,
Which made poor Simon whistle.

Verse 5:
He went for water in a sieve,
But soon it all fell through;
And now poor Simple Simon
Bids you all adieu.

She'll Be Comin' 'Round The Mountain

Traditional

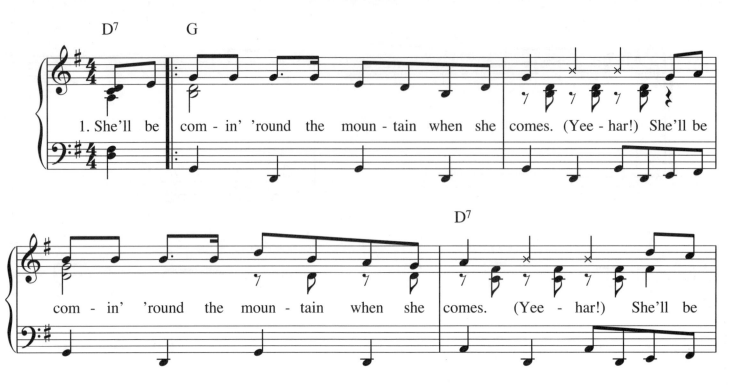

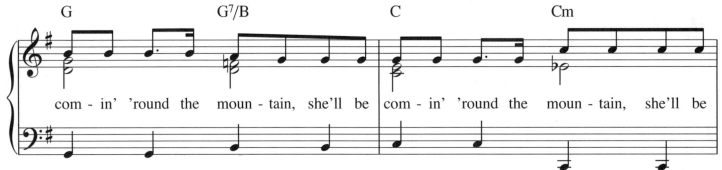

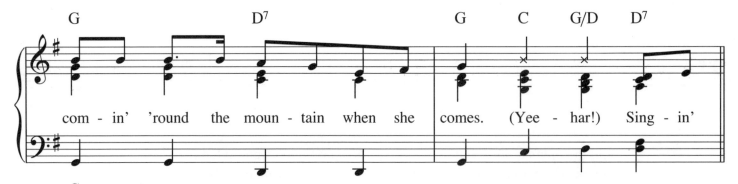

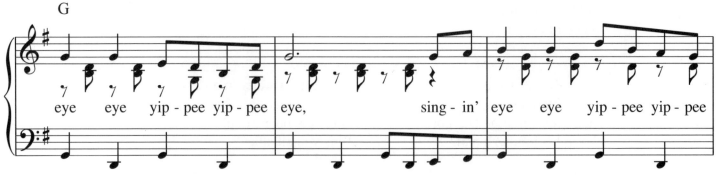

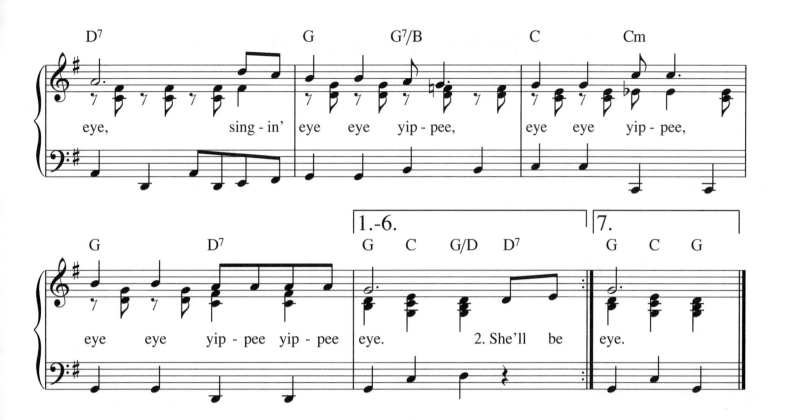

Chorus:
Singin' eye eye yippee yippee eye,
Singin' eye eye yippee yippee eye,
Singin' eye eye yippee,
Eye eye yippee,
Eye eye yippee yippee eye,

Verse 2:
She'll be ridin' six white horses when she comes.
(Whoa back!) *etc.*

Verse 3:
Oh we'll all come out to meet her when she comes.
(Hi, babe!) *etc.*

Verse 4:
She'll be wearin' pink pyjamas when she comes.
(Wolf whistle) *etc.*

Verse 5:
Oh we'll have to sleep with Grandma when she comes.
(Snore snore!) *etc.*

Verse 6:
Oh we'll all have chicken and dumplings when she comes.
(Yum yum!) *etc.*

Verse 7:
Oh we'll kill the old red rooster when she comes.
(Chop chop!) *etc.*

Short'nin' Bread

Traditional

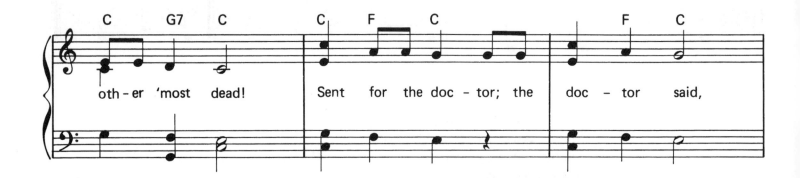

Three lit-tle chil-dren ly-in' in bed; Two were sick and the

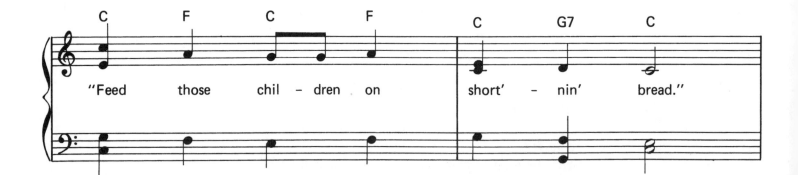

oth-er 'most dead! Sent for the doc-tor; the doc-tor said,

"Feed those chil-dren on short'-nin' bread."

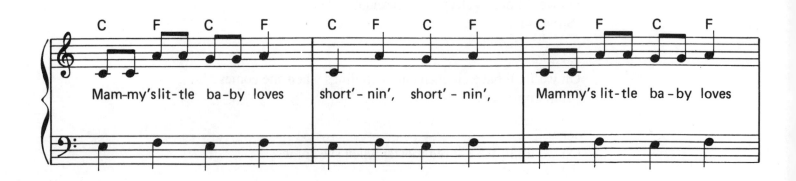

Mam-my's lit-tle ba-by loves short'-nin', short'-nin', Mammy's lit-tle ba-by loves

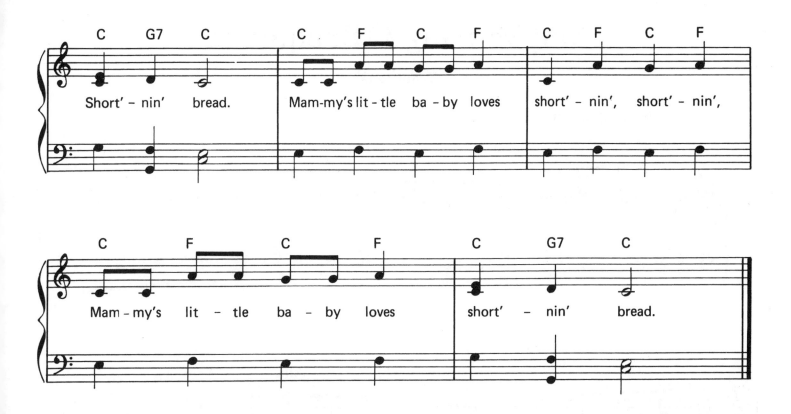

Verse 2:
Put in the skillet, put on the lid,
Mammy's gonna bake a little short'nin' bread.
That ain't all she's gonna do,
Mammy's gonna make a little coffee too.

Mammy's little baby loves short'nin', short'nin', *etc.*

Verse 3:
Then the little child, sick in bed,
When he hear tell of short'nin' bread,
Popped up well, he dance an' sing,
He almos' cut the pigeon wing.

Mammy's little baby loves short'nin', short'nin', *etc.*

Verse 4:
I slip to the kitchen, slip up the lid,
Filled mah pockets full of short'nin' bread,
Stole the skillet, stole the lid,
Stole the gal makin' short'nin' bread.

Mammy's little baby loves short'nin', short'nin', *etc.*

Verse 5:
They caught me with the skillet, they caught me with the lid,
They caught me with the gal makin' short'nin' bread,
Paid for the skillet, paid for the lid,
Spent six months in jail eatin' short'nin' bread.

Mammy's little baby loves short'nin', short'nin', *etc.*

Sing A Song Of Sixpence

Traditional

Moderately bright

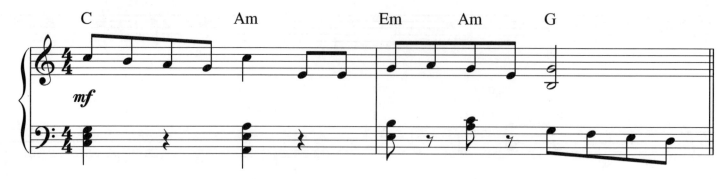

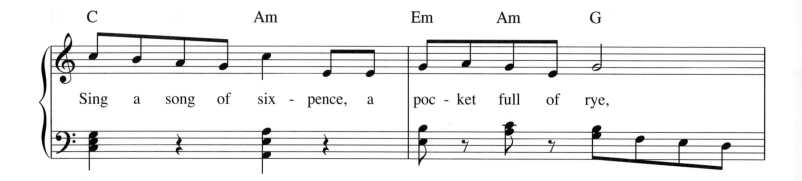

Sing a song of six - pence, a poc - ket full of rye,

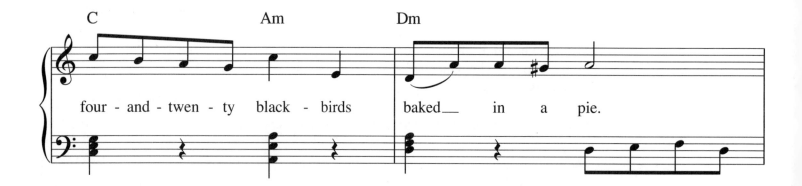

four - and - twen - ty black - birds baked__ in a pie.

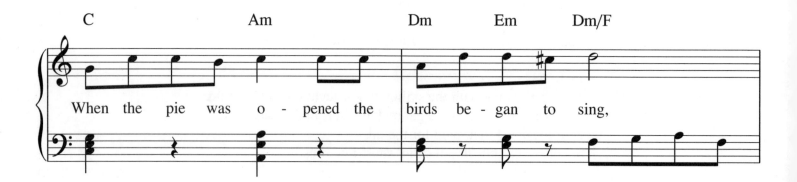

When the pie was o - pened the birds be - gan to sing,

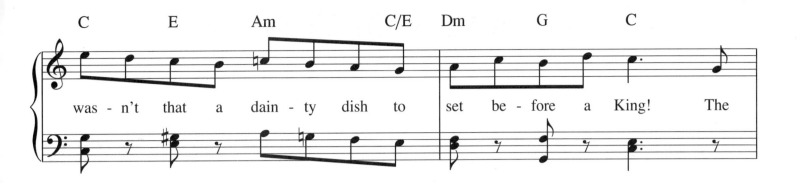

was-n't that a dain-ty dish to set be-fore a King! The

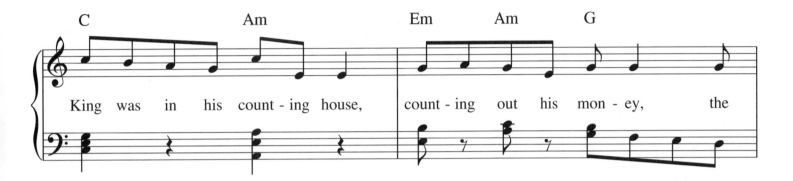

King was in his count-ing house, count-ing out his mon-ey, the

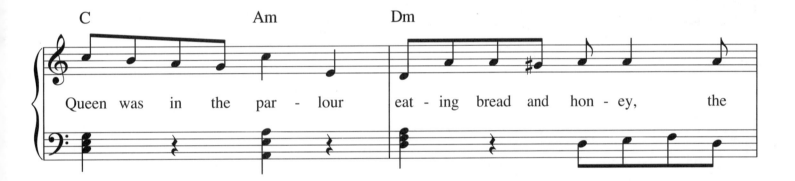

Queen was in the par-lour eat-ing bread and hon-ey, the

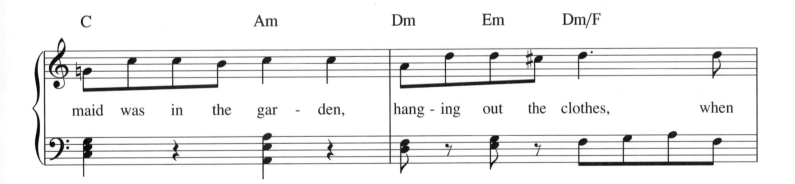

maid was in the gar-den, hang-ing out the clothes, when

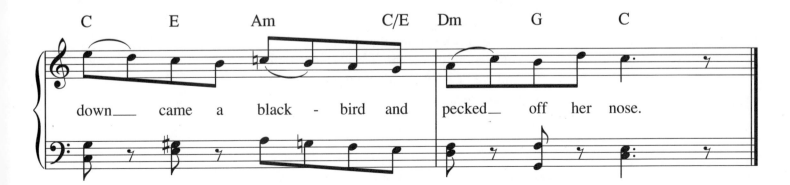

down___ came a black-bird and pecked___ off her nose.

Sleep, Baby, Sleep

Traditional

Lullaby

Sleep, baby, sleep. Your daddy's tending the

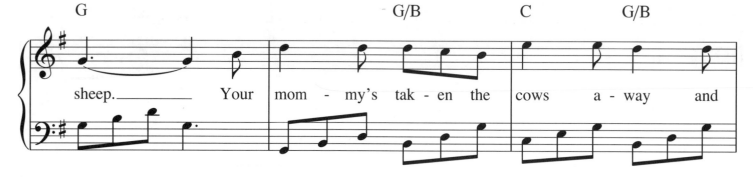

sheep. Your mommy's taken the cows away and

won't be home 'til the break of day. Sleep, baby, sleep.

Verse 2:
Sleep, baby, sleep.
Your daddy's tending the sheep.
Your mommy's tending the little ones;
Baby sleep as long as he wants.
Sleep, baby, sleep.

Verse 3:
Sleep, baby, sleep.
Your daddy's tending the sheep.
Your mommy's off too in gossiping flight
And won't be back 'til late tonight.
Sleep, baby, sleep.

Soldier, Soldier, Will You Marry Me?

Traditional

Moderately

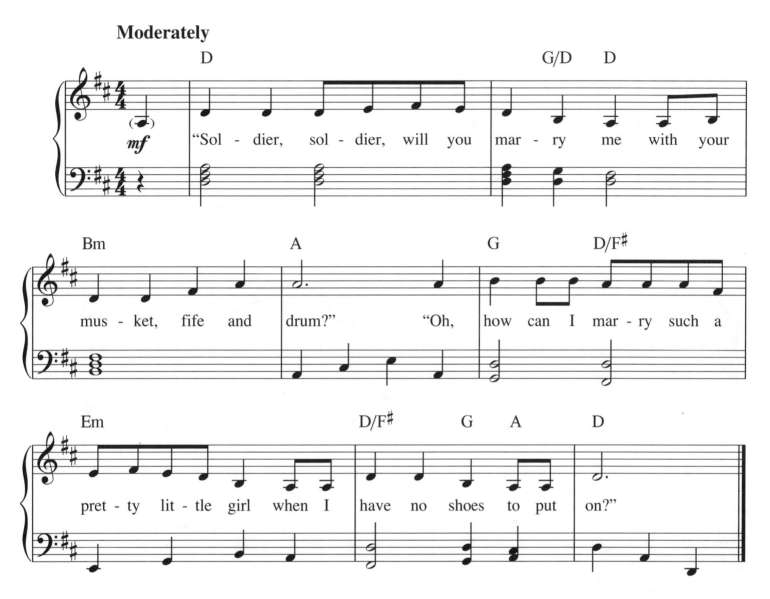

Verse 2:
Then off to the cobbler she did go as fast as she could run.
She brought him back the finest that was there, and the soldier put them on.

Verse 3:
"Now, soldier, soldier, will you marry me with your musket, fife and drum?"
"Oh, how can I marry such a pretty little girl when I have no coat to put on?"

Verse 4:
Then off to the tailor she did go as fast as she could run.
She brought him back the finest that was there, and the soldier put it on.

Verse 5:
"Now, soldier, soldier, will you marry me with your musket, fife and drum?"
"Oh, how can I marry such a pretty little girl when I've a good wife and baby at home?"

Skip To My Lou

Traditional

Lou,   Lou,   Skip to my Lou,   Lou,   Lou,   Skip to my Lou,

Lou,   Lou,   Skip to my Lou,   Skip to my Lou, my   dar - ling.

1. Lost my part - ner, What - 'll I do?   Lost my part - ner, what - 'll I do?

Lost my part - ner, What - 'll I do?   Skip to my Lou, my   dar - ling.

Sur Le Pont D'Avignon

Traditional

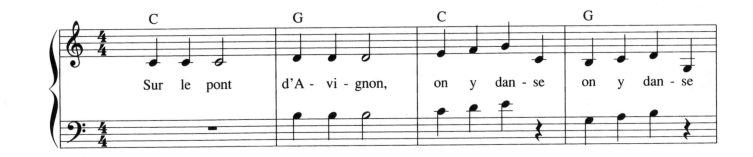

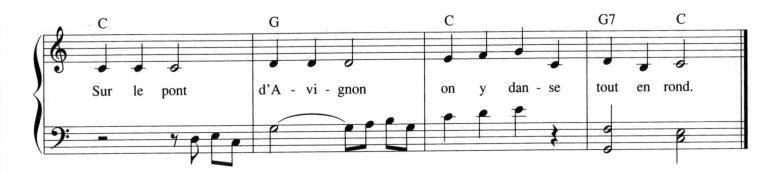

Teddy Bear, Teddy Bear

Traditional

Like a lullaby

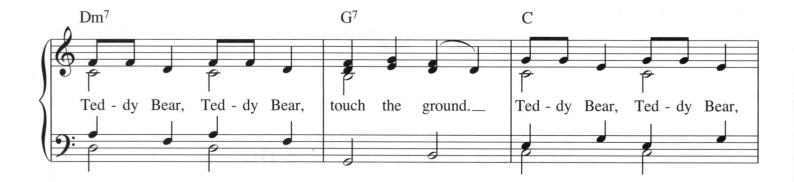

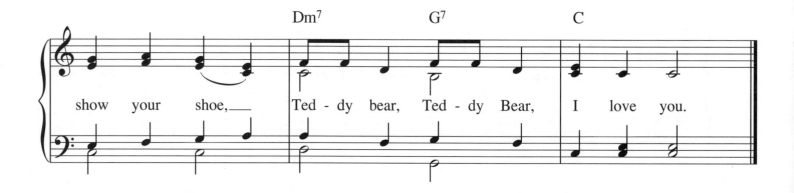

Verse 2:
Teddy Bear, Teddy Bear, climb the stairs,
Teddy Bear, Teddy Bear, say your prayers,
Teddy Bear, Teddy Bear, turn off the light,
Teddy Bear, Teddy Bear, say good night.

Ten Green Bottles

Traditional

Bouncy

(music notation for "Ten green bottles hanging on the wall. Ten green bottles hanging on the wall, and if one green bottle should accidenta'ly fall there'll be nine green bottles hanging on the wall.")

Verse 2:
Nine green bottles hanging on the wall.
Nine green bottles hanging on the wall.
And if one green bottle should accidenta'ly fall
There'll be eight green bottles hanging on the wall.

Verse 3:
Eight green bottles hanging on the wall. *etc.*

Verse 4:
Seven green bottles hanging on the wall. *etc.*

Verse 5:
Six green bottles hanging on the wall. *etc.*

Verse 6:
Five green bottles hanging on the wall. *etc.*

Verse 7:
Four green bottles hanging on the wall. *etc.*

Verse 8:
Three green bottles hanging on the wall. *etc.*

Verse 9:
Two green bottles hanging on the wall. *etc.*

Verse 10:
One green bottle hanging on the wall.
One green bottle hanging on the wall.
And if that green bottle should accidenta'ly fall
There'll be no green bottles hanging on the wall.

Ten Little Pigs

Traditional

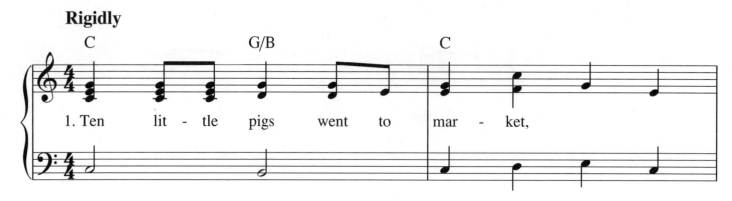

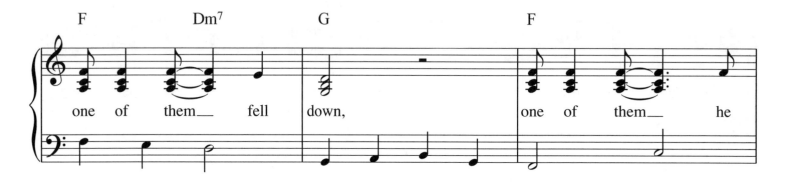

Verse 2:
Eight little pigs went to market,
One of them fell down,
One of them he ran away,
How many got to town?
Six!

Verse 3:
Six little pigs went to market,
One of them fell down,
One of them he ran away,
How many got to town?
Four!

Verse 4:
Four little pigs went to market,
One of them fell down,
One of them he ran away,
How many got to town?
Two!

Verse 5:
Two little pigs went to market,
One of them fell down,
One of them he ran away,
How many got to town?
None!

The Barnyard Song

Traditional

Verse 2:
I had a hen, and the hen pleased me,
I fed my hen under yonder tree;
Hen goes chimmy chuck, chimmy chuck,
Cat goes fiddle dee dee.

Verse 3:
I had a duck, *etc.*
...Duck goes quack, quack, *etc.*

Verse 4:
I had a pig, *etc.*
...Pig goes oink, oink, *etc.*

Verse 5:
I had a sheep, *etc.*
...Sheep goes baaa, baaa, *etc.*

Verse 6:
I had a turkey, *etc.*
...Turkey goes gibble-gobble, *etc.*

The Ants Came Marching

Traditional

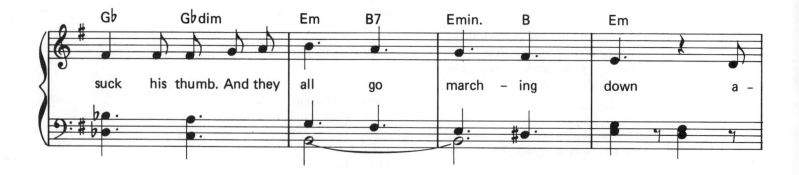

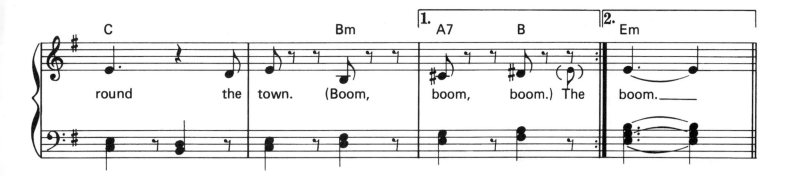

round the town. (Boom, boom, boom.) The boom.____

Verse 2:
The ants came marching two by two; Hurrah! Hurrah!
The ants came marching two by two; Hurrah! Hurrah!
The ants came marching two by two,
The little one stopped to tie his shoe,
And they all go marching down around the town.
(Boom, boom, boom.)

Verse 3:
The ants came marching three by three; Hurrah! Hurrah!
The ants came marching three by three; Hurrah! Hurrah!
The ants came marching three by three,
The little one stopped to climb a tree,
And they all go marching down around the town.
(Boom, boom, boom.)

Verse 4:
The ants came marching four by four…
The little one stopped to shut the door…

Verse 5:
The ants came marching five by five…
The little one stopped to take a dive…

Verse 6:
The ants came marching six by six…
The little one stopped to pick up sticks…

Verse 7:
The ants came marching seven by seven…
The little one stopped to go to heaven…

Verse 8:
The ants came marching eight by eight…
The little one stopped to shut the gate…

Verse 9:
The ants came marching nine by nine…
The little one stopped to scratch his spine…

Verse 10:
The ants came marching ten by ten…
The little one stopped to say "the end"…

The Bear Went Over The Mountain

Traditional

Moderately

Oh, the bear went o - ver the

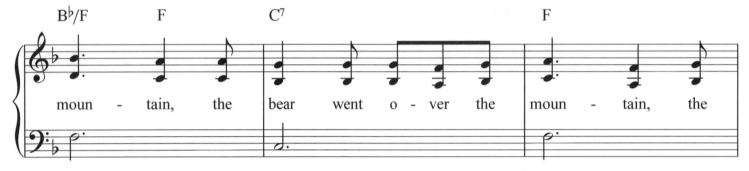

moun - tain, the bear went o - ver the moun - tain, the

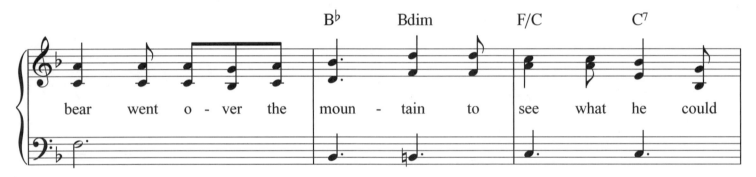

bear went o - ver the moun - tain to see what he could

see. To see what he could see,_____ to

see what he could see. Oh, the bear went o - ver the

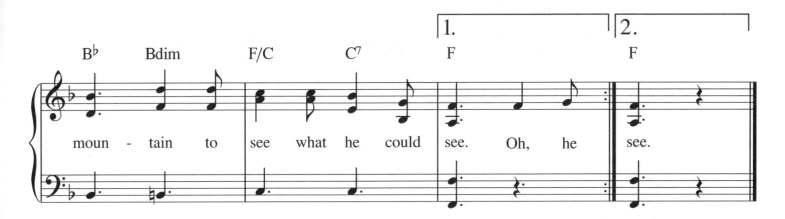

moun - tain to see what he could see. Oh, he see.

Verse 2:
Oh, he saw another mountain,
He saw another mountain,
He saw another mountain and that's what he could see.
And that's what he could see,
And that's what he could see,
Oh, he saw another mountain and that's what he could see.

Ten Little Indians

Traditional

One lit - tle, two lit - tle, three lit - tle In - di - ans

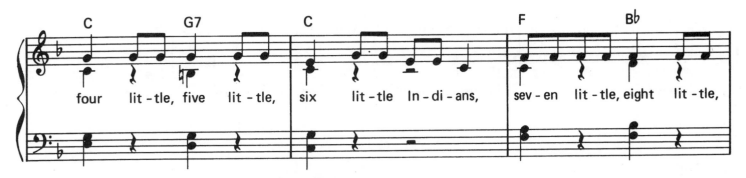

four lit - tle, five lit - tle, six lit - tle In - di - ans, sev - en lit - tle, eight lit - tle,

nine lit - tle In - di - ans, ten lit - tle In - di - an boys.

The Drunken Sailor

Traditional

With movement

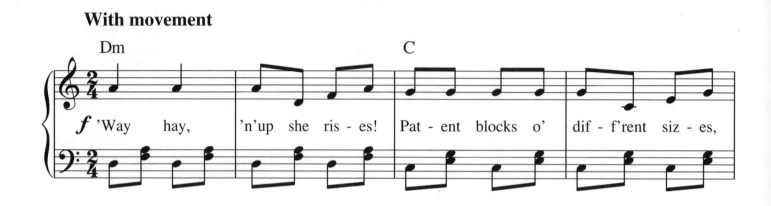

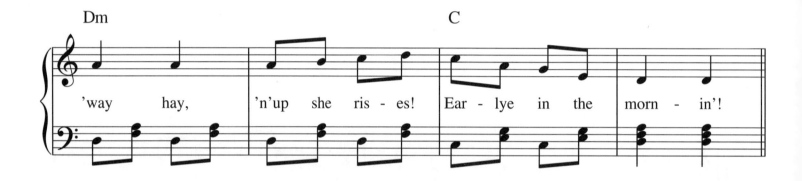

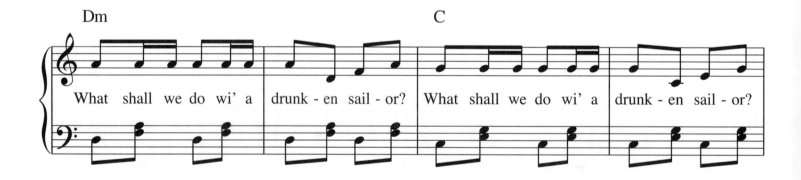

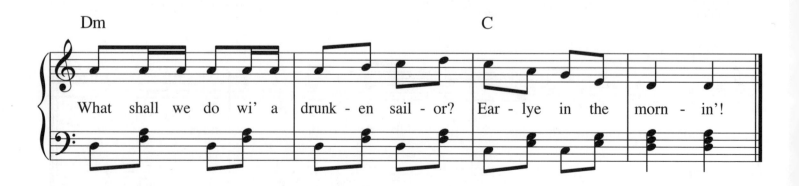

'Way hay, 'n' up she rises!
Patent blocks o' diff'rent sizes,
'Way hay 'n' up she rises!
Earlye in the mornin'!

Verse 2:
Put him in the long boat 'til he gets sober,
Put him in the long boat 'til he gets sober,
Put him in the long boat 'til he gets sober,
Earlye in the mornin'!

'Way hay, 'n' up she rises! *etc.*

Verse 3:
Keep him there an' make him bail her,
Keep him there an' make him bail her,
Keep him there an' make him bail her,
Earlye in the mornin'!

'Way hay, 'n' up she rises! *etc.*

Verse 4:
Trice him up in a runnin' bowline,
Trice him up in a runnin' bowline,
Trice him up in a runnin' bowline,
Earlye in the mornin'!

'Way hay, 'n' up she rises! *etc.*

Verse 5:
Tie him to the taffrail when she's yardarm under,
Tie him to the taffrail when she's yardarm under,
Tie him to the taffrail when she's yardarm under,
Earlye in the mornin'!

'Way hay, 'n' up she rises! *etc.*

Verse 6:
Put him in the scuppers with a hosepipe on him,
Put him in the scuppers with a hosepipe on him,
Put him in the scuppers with a hosepipe on him,
Earlye in the mornin'!

'Way hay, 'n' up she rises! *etc.*

Verse 7:
Take 'im an' shake 'im, an' try an' wake 'im,
Take 'im an' shake 'im, an' try an' wake 'im,
Take 'im an' shake 'im, an' try an' wake 'im,
Earlye in the mornin'!

'Way hay, 'n' up she rises! *etc.*

Verse 8:
Give him a dose o' salt an' water,
Give him a dose o' salt an' water,
Give him a dose o' salt an' water,
Earlye in the mornin'!

'Way hay, 'n' up she rises! *etc.*

Verse 9:
Give him a taste o' the bosun's rope-end,
Give him a taste o' the bosun's rope-end,
Give him a taste o' the bosun's rope-end,
Earlye in the mornin'!

'Way hay, 'n' up she rises! *etc.*

The Farmer In The Dell

Traditional

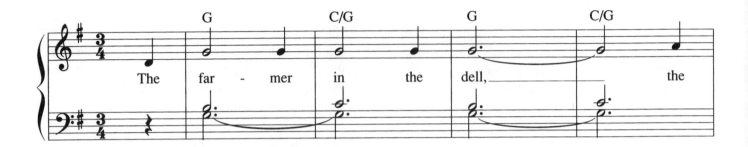

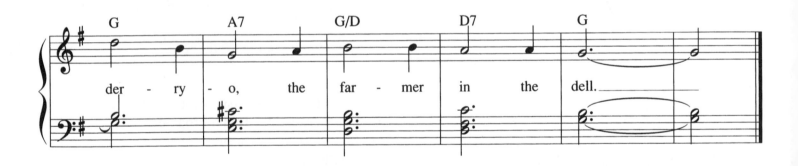

Verse 2:
The farmer takes a wife *etc.*

Verse 3:
The wife takes a child *etc.*

Verse 4:
The child takes a nurse *etc.*

Verse 5:
The nurse takes a dog *etc.*

Verse 6:
The dog takes a cat *etc.*

Verse 7:
The cat takes a rat *etc.*

Verse 8:
The rat takes a cheese *etc.*

Verse 9:
The cheese stands alone *etc.*

The Grand Old Duke Of York

Traditional

Brightly

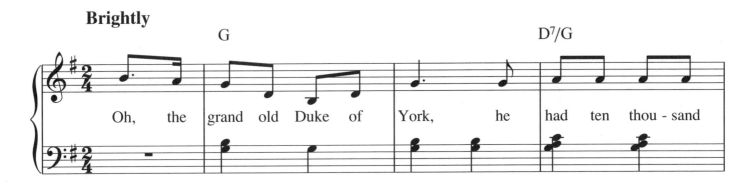

Oh, the grand old Duke of York, he had ten thou-sand

men, he marched them up to the top of the hill and he

marched them down a - gain, and_____ when they were up, they were

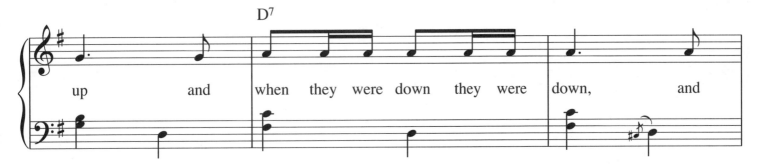

up and when they were down they were down, and

when they were on - ly half way up they were nei - ther up nor down.

The Muffin Man

Traditional

Do you know the Muf - fin Man, the Muf - fin Man, the Muf - fin Man? Oh,

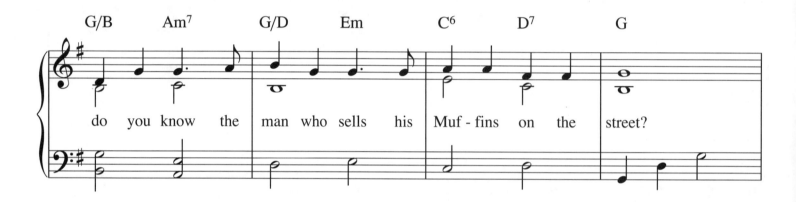

do you know the man who sells his Muf - fins on the street?

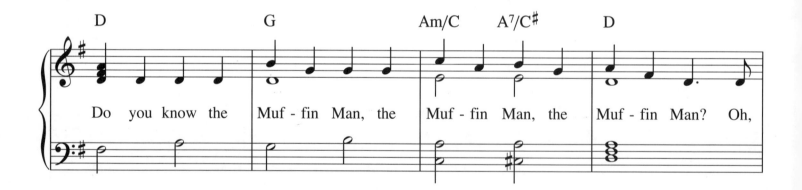

Do you know the Muf - fin Man, the Muf - fin Man, the Muf - fin Man? Oh,

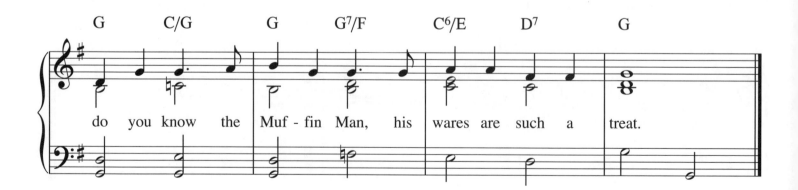

do you know the Muf - fin Man, his wares are such a treat.

The Music Man

Traditional

Verse 2:
I am the music man,
I come from far away,
And I can play.
What can you play?
I play the bass drum.

Boom-di, boom-di, boom-di-boom,
Boom-di-boom, boom-di-boom,
Boom-di, boom-di, boom-di-boom,
Boom-di, boom-di-boom.
Pi-a, pi-a, pi-a-no, *etc.*

Verse 3:
I am the music man,
I come from far away,
And I can play.
What can you play?
I play the trumpet.

Toot-ti, toot-ti, toot-ti-toot,
Toot-ti-toot, toot-ti-toot,
Toot-ti, toot-ti, toot-ti-toot,
Toot-ti, toot-ti-toot.
Boom-di, boom-di, boom-di-boom, *etc.*
Pia-a, pi-a, pi-a-no, *etc.*

The North Wind Doth Blow

Traditional

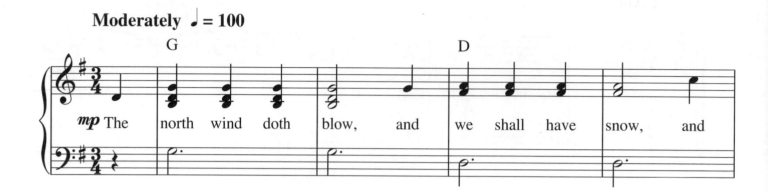

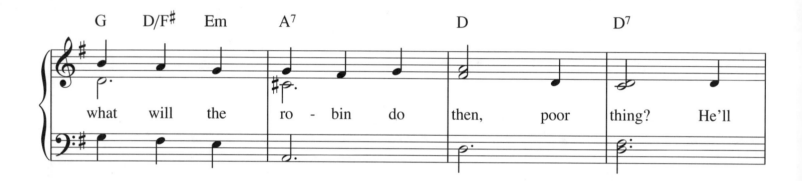

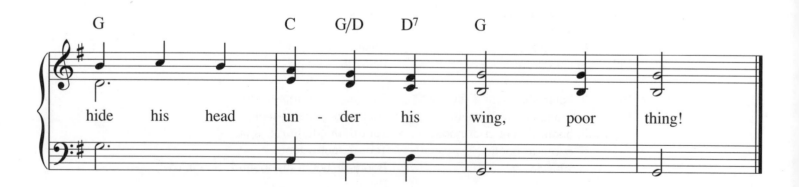

The Rainbow Song

Traditional

The Quartermaster's Store

Traditional

Quick march

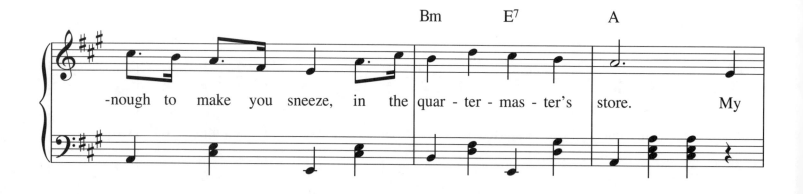

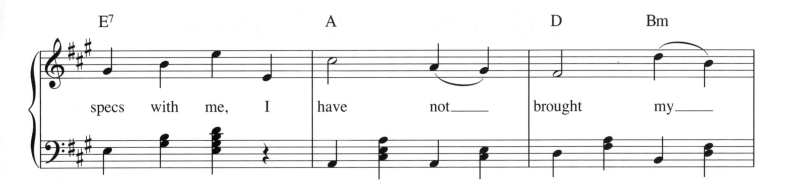

specs with me, I have not___ brought my___

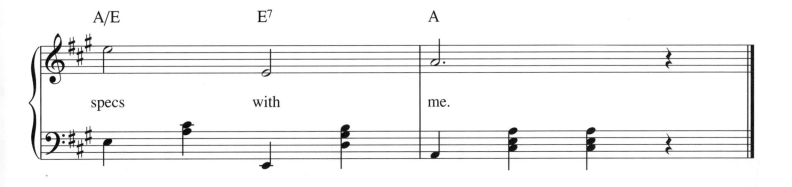

specs with me.

Verse 2:
There were rats, rats,
As big as bloomin' cats,
In the store, in the store.
There were rats, rats,
As big as bloomin' cats,
In the quartermaster's store.
My eyes are dim, I cannot see,
I have not brought my specs with me,
I have not brought my specs with me.

Verse 3:
There was bread, bread,
Harder than your head,
In the store, in the store.
There was bread, bread,
Harder than your head,
In the quartermaster's store.
My eyes are dim, I cannot see,
I have not brought my specs with me,
I have not brought my specs with me.

The Owl And The Pussycat

Traditional

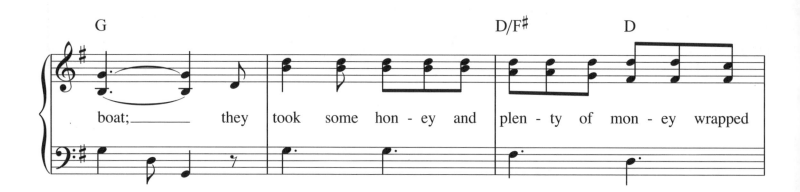

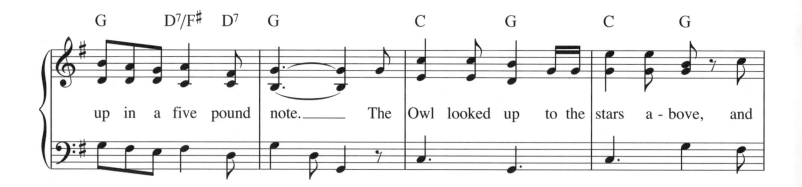

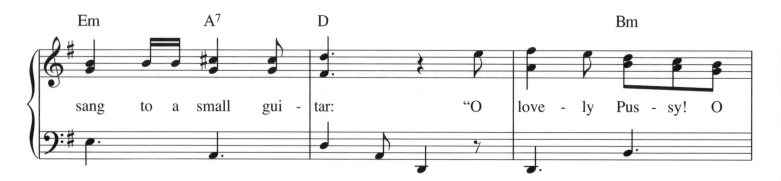

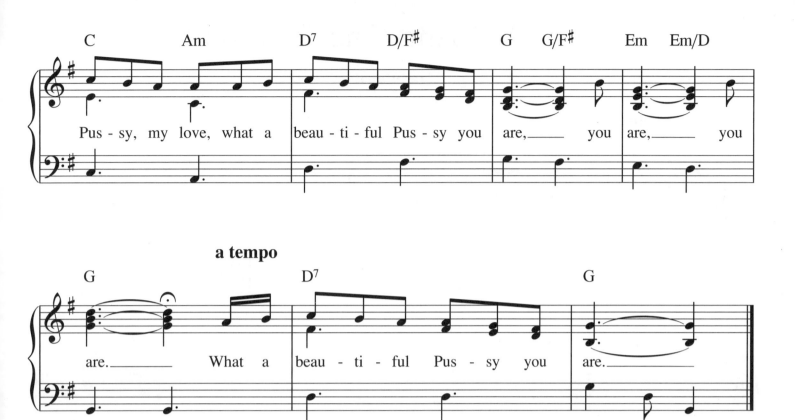

C Am D⁷ D/F♯ G G/F♯ Em Em/D

Pus - sy, my love, what a beau - ti - ful Pus - sy you are,____ you are,____ you

a tempo

G D⁷ G

are._____ What a beau - ti - ful Pus - sy you are._____

Verse 2:
Pussy said to the Owl: "You elegant fowl,
How charmingly sweet you sing!
Oh, let us be married; too long we have tarried;
But what shall we do for a ring?"
They sailed away for a year and a day
To the land where the bong tree grows;
And there in the woods, a piggy-wig stood
With a ring at the end of his nose,
His nose,
His nose,
With a ring at the end of his nose.

Verse 3:
"Dear Pig, are you willing to sell for one shilling
Your ring?" Said the piggy, "I will."
So they took it away, and were married next day
By the turkey who lives on the hill.
They dined on mince and slices of quince,
Which they ate with a runcible spoon,
And hand in hand on the edge of the sand,
They danced by the light of the moon,
The moon,
The moon,
They danced by the light of the moon.

The Wheels On The Bus

Traditional

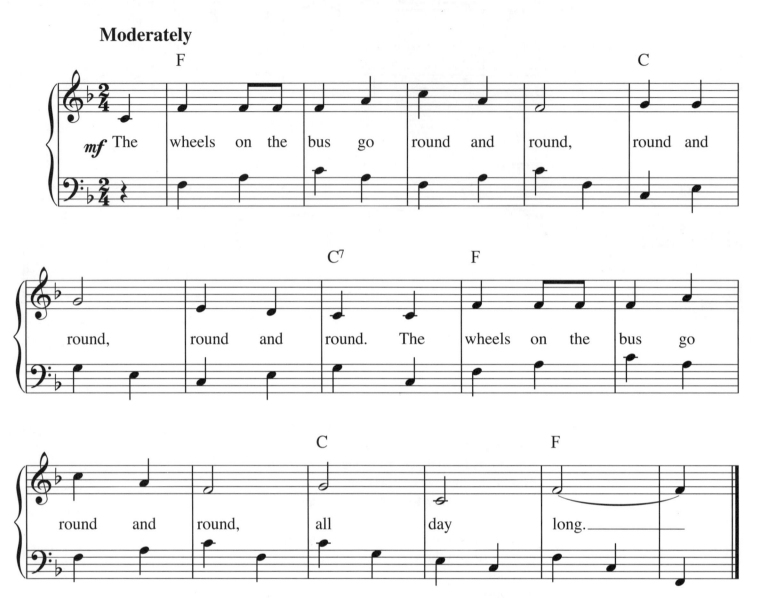

Verse 2:
The wipers on the bus go swish, swish, swish,
Swish, swish, swish, *etc.*

Verse 3:
The horn on the bus goes beep, beep, beep,
Beep, beep, beep, *etc.*

Verse 4:
The children on the bus go chatter, chatter, chatter,
Chatter, chatter, chatter, *etc.*

Verse 5:
The people on the bus bounce up and down,
Up and down, up and down, *etc.*

Verse 6:
The babies on the bus fall fast asleep,
Fast asleep, fast asleep, *etc.*

There Was A Crooked Man

Traditional

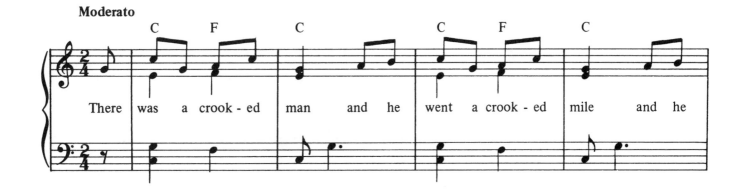

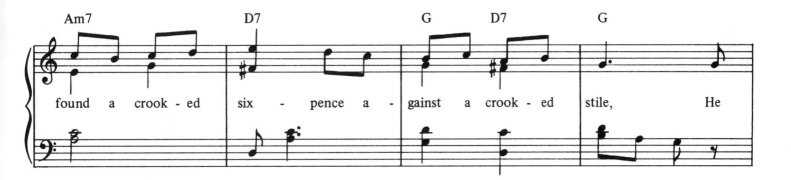

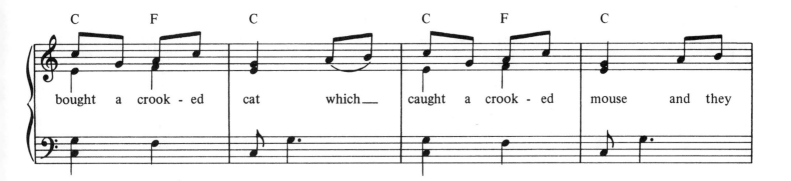

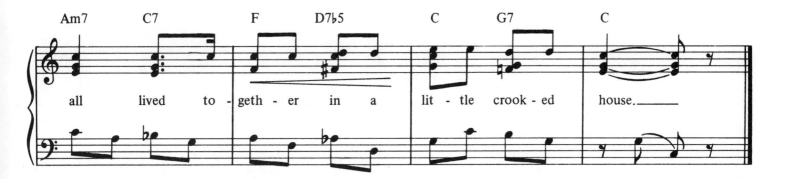

There Was An Old Frog

Traditional

Moderately

1. There was an old frog and he lived in the spring,

mf

(Verses 2 - 4 see block lyric)

Ching - a chang - a pol - ly mitch - a cow - me - o, He was so hoarse he

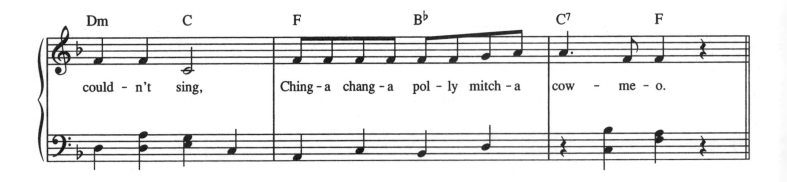

could - n't sing, Ching - a chang - a pol - ly mitch - a cow - me - o.

Refrain

Kee - mo ky - mo do - ro war, May - hi, may - lo, my

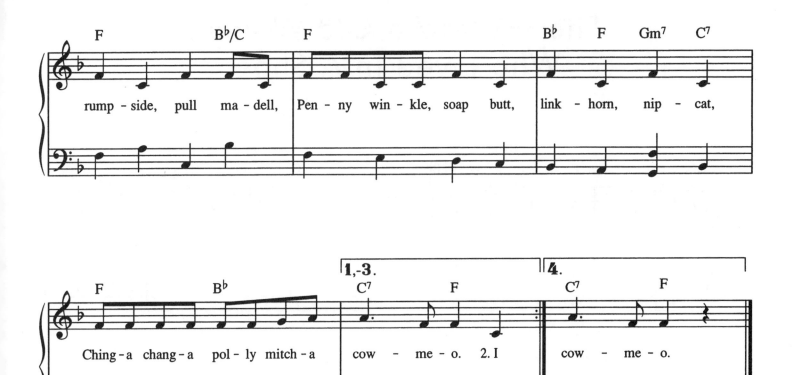

Verse 2:
I grabbed him by the leg and pulled him out,
Ching-a-chang-a-polly mitch-a-cow-me-o,
He hopped and he skipped and he bounced all about,
Ching-a-chang-a-polly mitch-a-cow-me-o.

Keemo kymo doro war, *etc.*

Verse 3:
Cheese in the spring house nine days old,
Ching-a-chang-a-polly mitch-a-cow-me-o,
Rats and skippers is a-getting mighty bold,
Ching-a-chang-a-polly mitch-a-cow-me-o.

Keemo kymo doro war, *etc.*

Verse 4:
Big fat rat and a bucket of souse,
Ching-a-chang-a-polly mitch-a-cow-me-o,
Take it back to the big white house,
Ching-a-chang-a-polly mitch-a-cow-me-o.

Keemo kymo doro war, *etc.*

There Was An Old Woman
Who Lived In A Shoe

Traditional

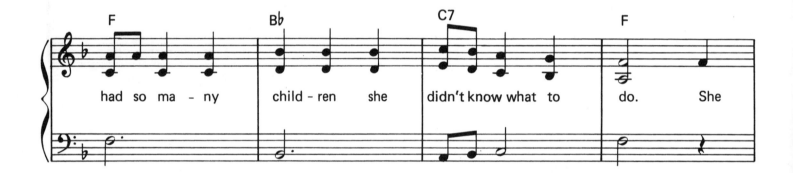

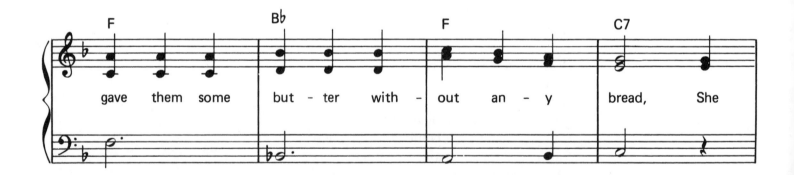

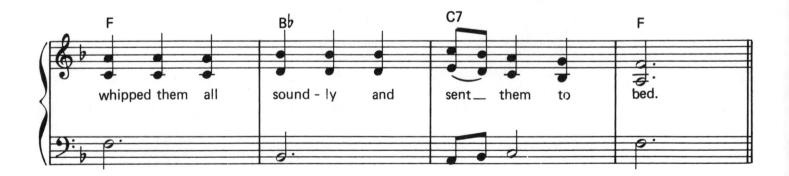

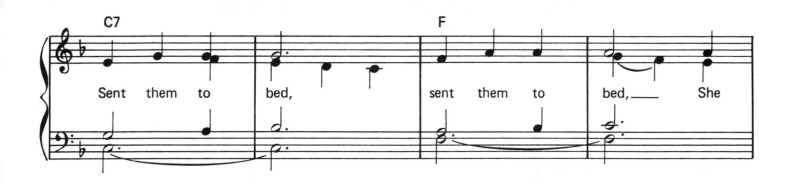

Sent them to bed, sent them to bed,___ She

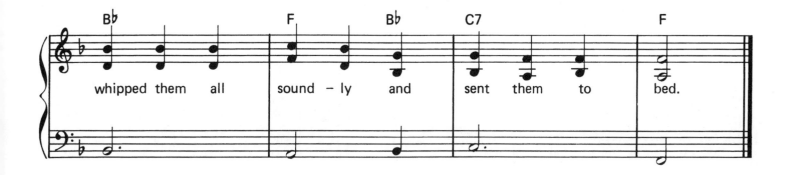

whipped them all sound – ly and sent them to bed.

Verse 2:
Then all those poor children crept under the clothes,
The cold pinched their fingers and also their toes,
And eating their butter without any bread,
Was not very nice for supper, they said.
Supper they said, supper they said,
Was not very nice for supper, they said.

Verse 3:
And then the old woman who lived in the shoe,
She felt so very sorry she didn't know what to do,
She ran to the bakers to get them some bread,
And kissed them all sweetly and then they were fed.
Then they were fed, then they were fed.
And kissed them all sweetly and then they were fed.

There Was An Old Man

Traditional

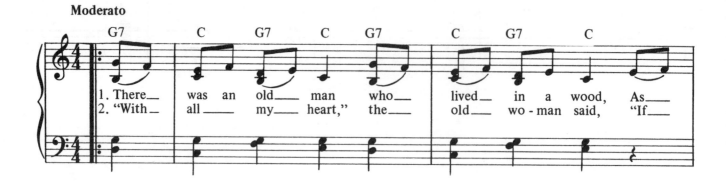

Verse 3:
"But you must milk the Tidy cow,
For fear that she go dry;
And you must feed the little pigs
That are within the sty.

Verse 4:
And you must mind the speckled hen,
For fear she lay away;
And you must reel a spool of yarn
That I spun yesterday."

Verse 5:
The old woman took a staff in her hand
And went to drive the plough;
The old man took a pail in his hand,
And went to milk the cow.

Verse 6:
But Tidy hinched and Tidy flinched,
And Tidy broke his nose;
And Tidy gave him such a blow
That blood ran down to his toes.

Verse 7:
"Hi Tidy! Ho Tidy! High!
Tidy do stand still!
If ever I milk you, Tidy, again,
'Twill be sore against my will!"

There Was A Princess

Traditional

Moderately

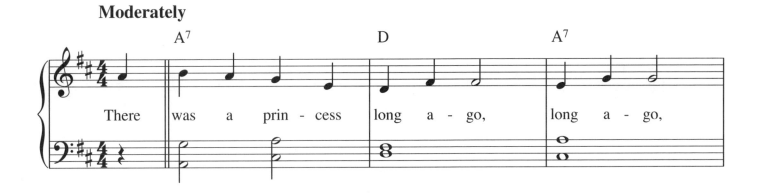

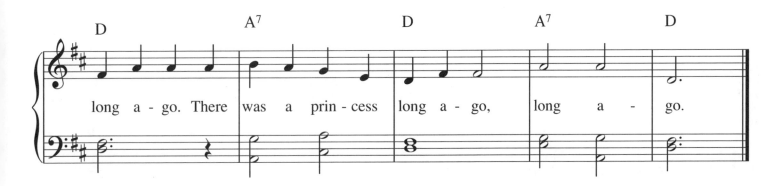

Verse 2:
And she lived in a big high tower,
Big high tower, big high tower,
And she lived in a big high tower,
Big high tower.

Verse 3:
One day a bad queen cast a spell,
Cast a spell, cast a spell,
One day a bad queen cast a spell,
Cast a spell.

Verse 4:
The princess slept for a hundred years, *etc.*

Verse 5:
A great big forest grew around, *etc.*

Verse 6:
A gallant prince came riding by, *etc.*

Verse 7:
He cut the trees down with his sword, *etc.*

Verse 8:
He woke the princess with a kiss, *etc.*

Verse 9:
So everybody's happy now, *etc.*

Activity suggestion:
Pick three children to play the princess, prince and queen. All other children form a circle and join hands.
The prince is on the outside of the circle, the princess and the queen on the inside. Whilst singing verse 1, the
children forming the circle walk around clockwise. Mime the actions for subsequent verses. In verse 6, the prince
skips around the outside of the circle and in verse 7, he breaks through the circle to join the princess.
For the final verse, everyone skips around clockwise.

There's A Hole In My Bucket

Traditional

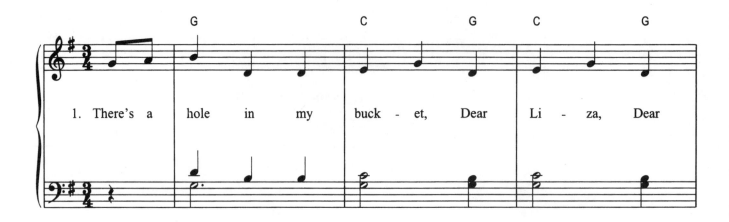

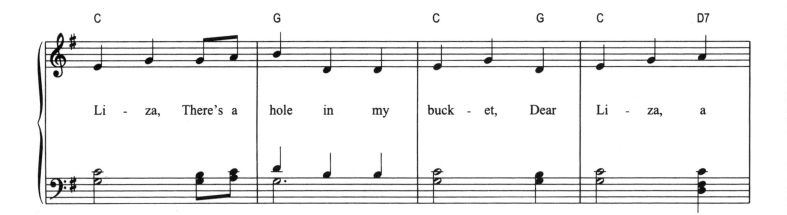

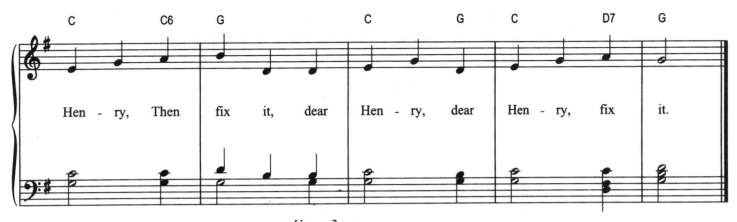

Hen - ry, Then fix it, dear Hen - ry, dear Hen - ry, fix it.

Verse 2:
With what shall I fix it?
Dear Liza, dear Liza,
With what shall I fix it?
Dear Liza, with what?

This Old Man

Moderately   Traditional

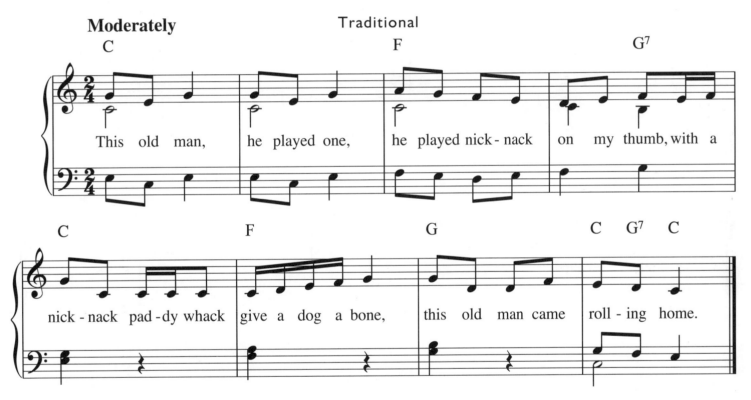

This old man, he played one, he played nick-nack on my thumb, with a nick-nack pad-dy whack give a dog a bone, this old man came roll-ing home.

Verse 2:
This old man, he played two,
He played nick-nack on my shoe, *etc.*

Verse 3:
This old man, he played three… knee, *etc.*

Verse 4:
This old man, he played four… door, *etc.*

Verse 5:
This old man, he played five… hive, *etc.*

Verse 6:
This old man, he played six… sticks, *etc.*

Verse 7:
This old man, he played seven… up in heaven, *etc.*

Verse 8:
This old man, he played eight… gate, *etc.*

Verse 9:
This old man, he played nine… spine, *etc.*

Verse 10:
This old man, he played ten… once again, *etc.*

There Were Ten In A Bed

Traditional

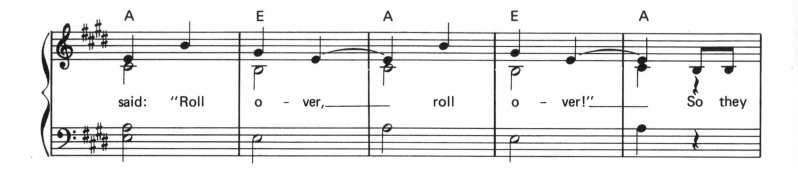

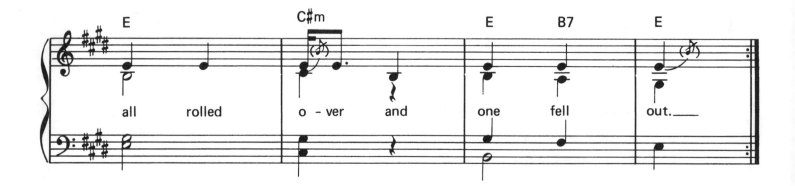

Verse 2:
There were nine in the bed, *etc.*

Verse 3:
There were eight in the bed, *etc.*

Verse 4:
There were seven in the bed, *etc.*

Verse 5:
There were six in the bed, *etc.*

Verse 6:
There were five in the bed, *etc.*

Verse 7:
There were four in the bed, *etc.*

Verse 8:
There were three in the bed, *etc.*

Verse 9:
There were two in the bed, *etc.*

Verse 10:
There was one in the bed, *etc.*
And the little one said, "Good night!"

This Little Pig Went To Market

Traditional

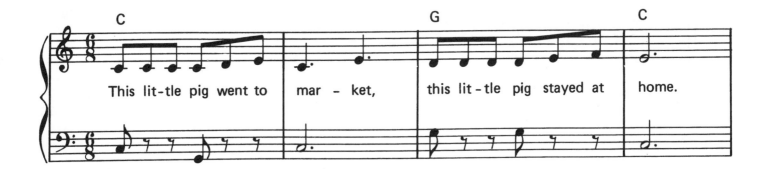

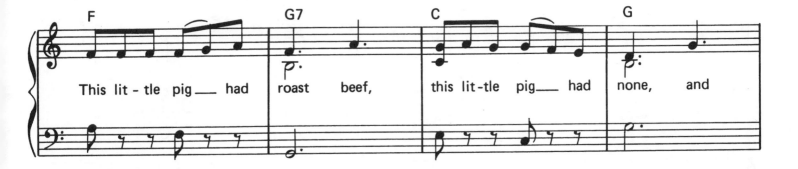

Three Blind Mice

Traditional

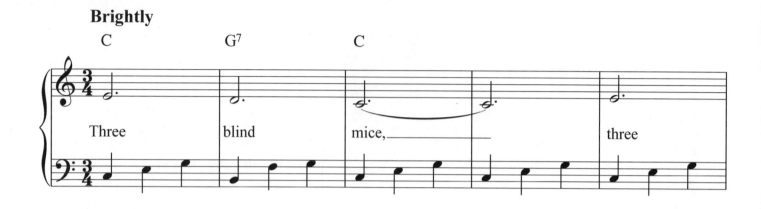

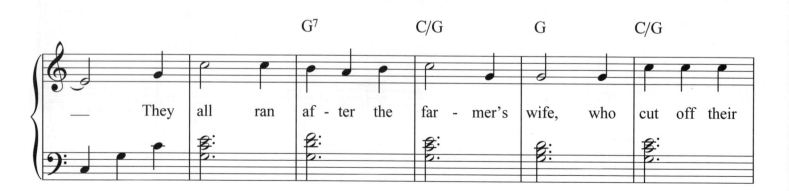

tails with a carv - ing knife. Did ev - er you see such a

thing in your life, as three blind mice?

Turn Again Whittington

Traditional

Stately

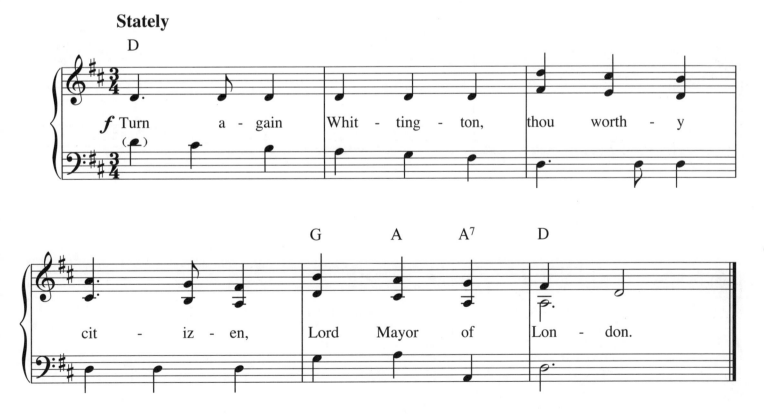

f Turn a - gain Whit - ting - ton, thou worth - y

cit - iz - en, Lord Mayor of Lon - don.

Three Little Kittens

Traditional

Once three lit-tle kit-tens They lost their mit-tens, And they be-gan to

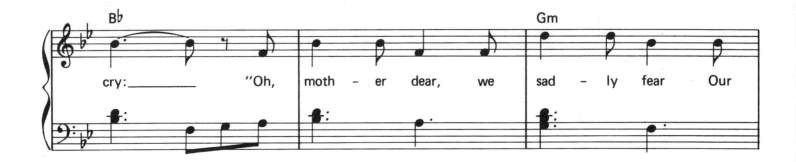

cry:_____ "Oh, moth-er dear, we sad-ly fear Our

mit-tens we have lost!"_____ "What! Lost your mit-tens! You

naugh-ty kit-tens! Then you shall have no pie."

Verse 2:
The three little kittens, they found their mittens,
And they began to cry:
"Oh, mother dear, see here, see here!
Our mittens we have found!"
"What? Found your mittens? You darling kittens!
Then you shall have some pie!"
"Meow, meow, meow, meow!"

Verse 3:
The three little kittens put on their mittens,
And soon ate up their pie,
"Oh, mother dear, we greatly fear,
Our mittens we have soiled!"
"What? Soiled your mittens? You naughty kittens!"
Then they began to sigh,
"Meow, meow, meow, meow!"

Verse 4:
The three little kittens, they washed their mittens,
And hung them up to dry.
"Oh, mother dear, look here, look here!
Our mittens we have washed!"
"What? Washed your mittens? You darling kittens!
But I smell a rat close by.
Hush, hush, hush, hush."

Tom, Tom, The Piper's Son

Traditional

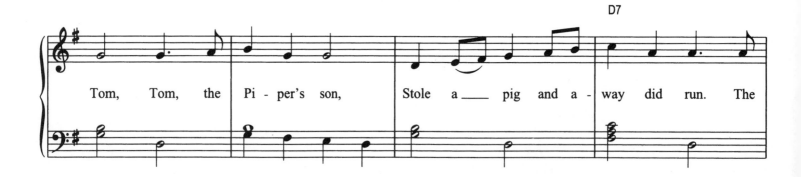

Tommy Thumb

Traditional

Bright

Verse 2:
Peter Pointer, Peter Pointer,
Where are you?
Here I am, here I am.
How do you do?

Verse 3:
Middle Man, Middle Man,
Where are you?
Here I am, here I am.
How do you do?

Verse 4:
Ruby Ring, Ruby Ring,
Where are you?
Here I am, here I am.
How do you do?

Verse 5:
Baby Small, Baby Small,
Where are you?
Here I am, here I am.
How do you do?

Verse 6:
Fingers all, fingers all,
Where are you?
Here we are, here we are.
How do you do?

Twinkle, Twinkle, Little Star

Traditional

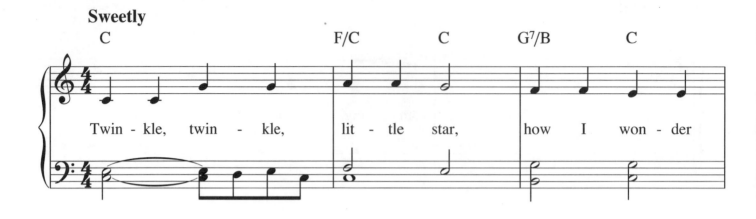

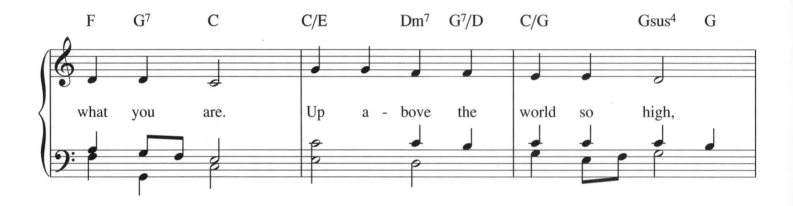

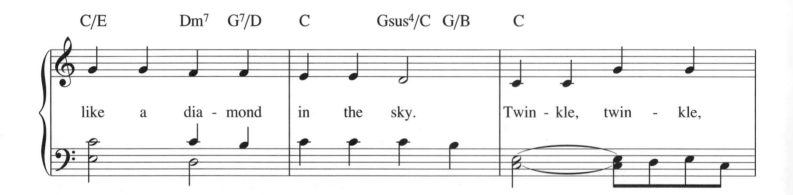

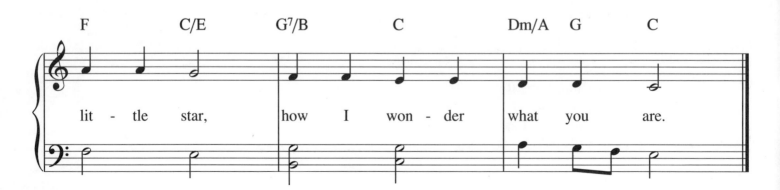

Two Little Chickens

Traditional

Moderately

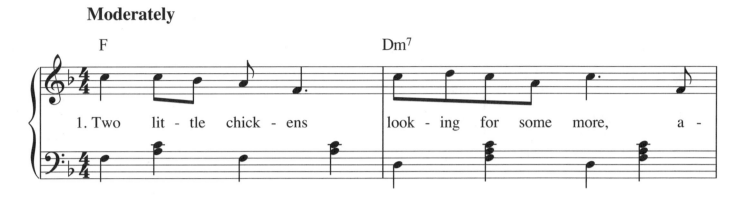

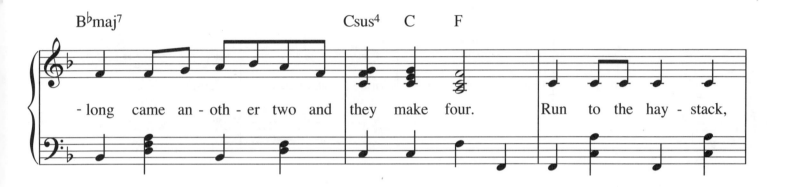

Verse 2:
Four little chickens getting in a fix,
Along came another two and they make six.
Run to the haystack, run to the pen,
Run little chickens, back to Mother Hen.

Verse 3:
Six little chickens perching on a gate,
Along came another two and they make eight.
Run to the haystack, run to the pen,
Run little chickens, back to Mother Hen.

Verse 4:
Eight little chickens run to Mother Hen,
Along came another two and they make ten.
Run to the haystack, run to the pen,
Run little chickens, back to Mother Hen.

Two Little Dickie Birds

Traditional

Two lit-tle dic-kie birds, sit-ting on a wall;___

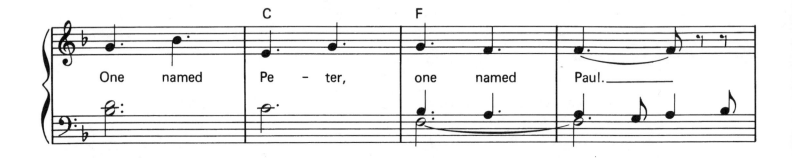

One named Pe-ter, one named Paul.___

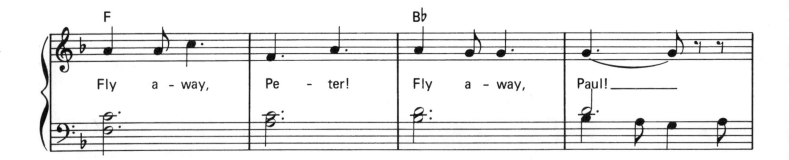

Fly a-way, Pe-ter! Fly a-way, Paul!___

Come back, Pe-ter! Come back, Paul!___

Underneath The Spreading Chestnut Tree

Traditional

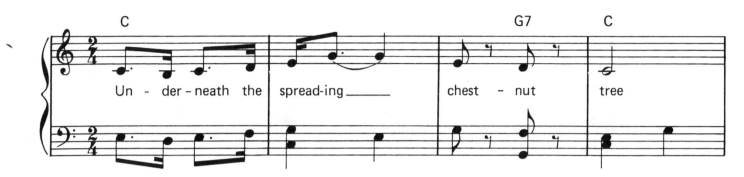

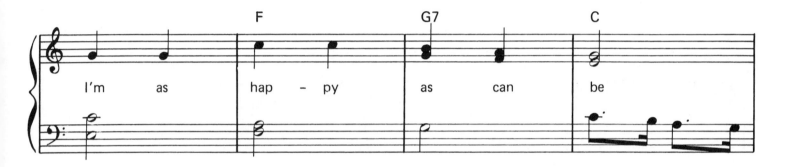

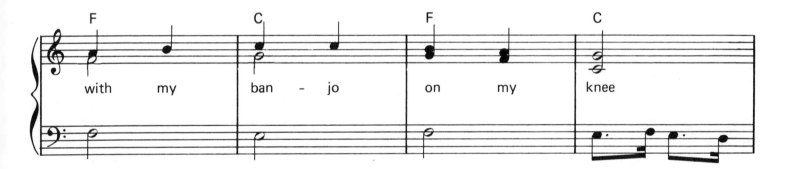

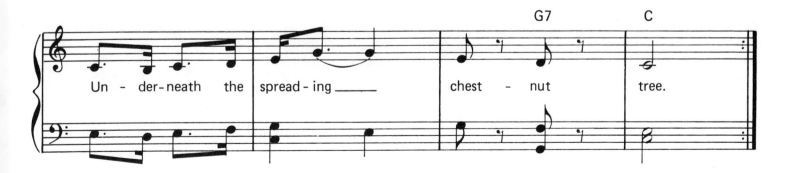

Wee Willie Winkie

Traditional

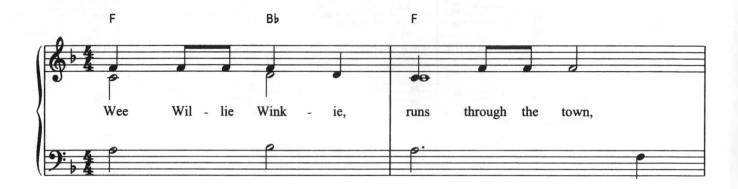

Wee Willie Winkie, runs through the town,
Upstairs and downstairs in his nightgown.
Rapping at the window,
Crying at the lock,
Are the children all in bed,
For now it's eight o'clock?

What Are Little Boys Made Of?

Traditional

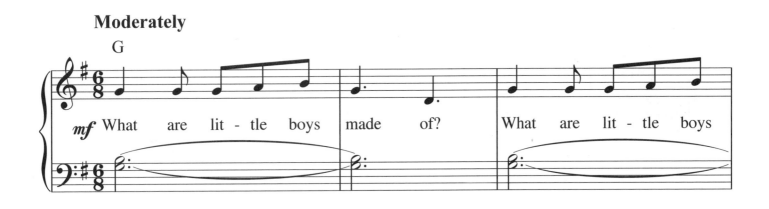

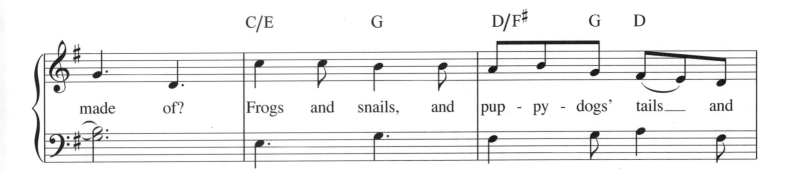

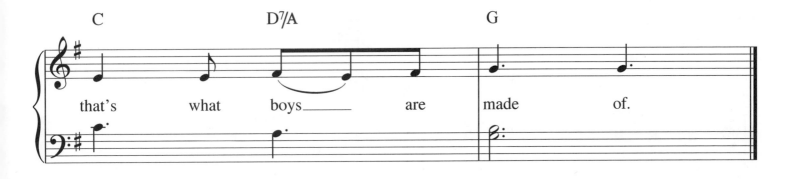

Verse 2:
What are little girls made of?
What are little girls made of?
Sugar and spice, and all things nice,
And that's what girls are made of.

When Johnny Comes Marching Home

Music by Patrick Sarsfield Gilmore

1. When John - ny comes march - ing home a - gain, hur - rah!_____ Hur -

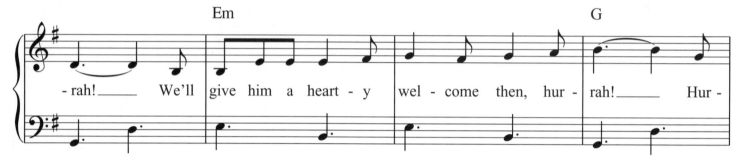

- rah!_____ We'll give him a heart - y wel - come then, hur - rah!_____ Hur -

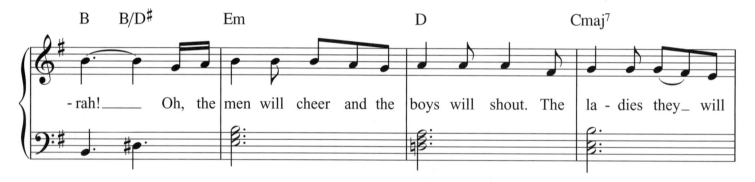

- rah!_____ Oh, the men will cheer and the boys will shout. The la - dies they___ will

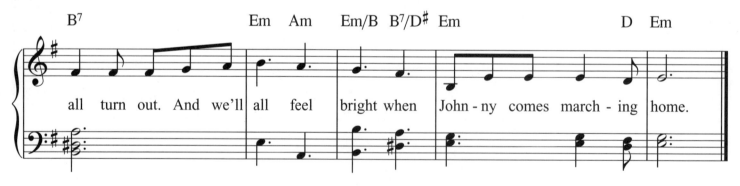

all turn out. And we'll all feel bright when John - ny comes march - ing home.

Verse 2:
Get ready for the Jubilee,
  hurrah! Hurrah!
We'll give the hero three times three,
  hurrah! Hurrah!
The laural wreath is ready now
To place upon his loyal brow.
And we'll all feel bright when
  Johnny comes marching home.

Verse 3:
The old church bell will peal with joy,
  hurrah! Hurrah!
To welcome home our darling boy,
  hurrah! Hurrah!
The village lads and lassies say,
With roses they will strew the way.
And we'll all feel bright when
  Johnny comes marching home.

Verse 4:
Let love and friendship on that day,
  hurrah! Hurrah!
Their choicest treasures then display,
  hurrah! Hurrah!
And let each one perform some part,
To fill with joy the warrior's heart.
And we'll all feel bright when
  Johnny comes marching home.

Where Are You Going To My Pretty Maid?

Traditional

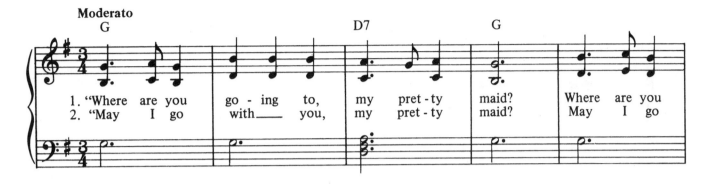

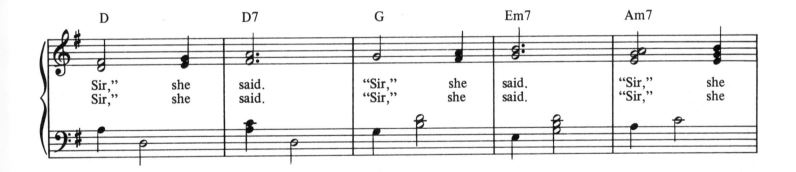

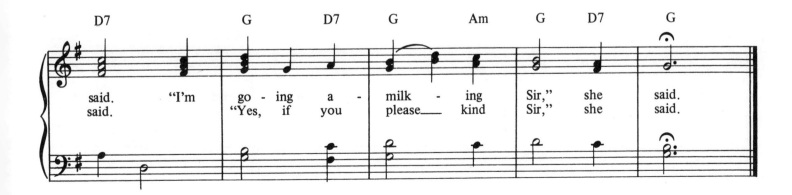

Who Killed Cock Robin?

Traditional

Slowly

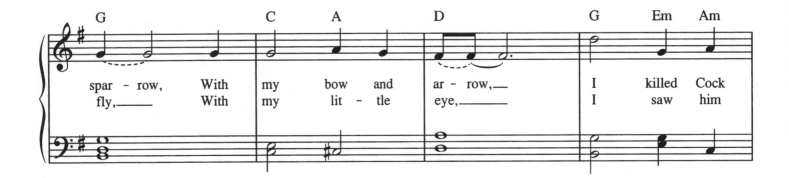

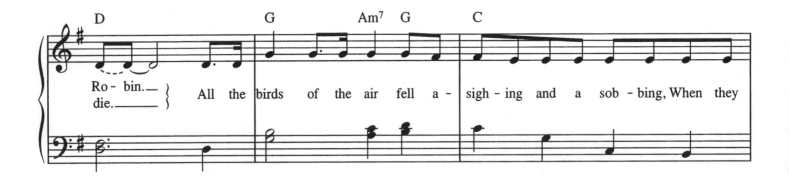

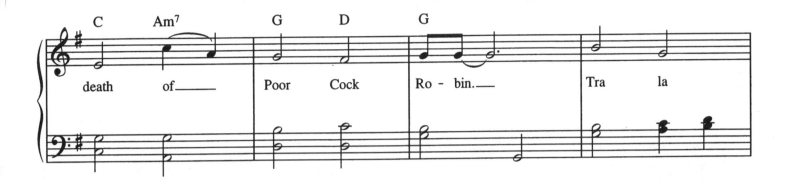

death of_____ Poor Cock Ro - bin.___ Tra la

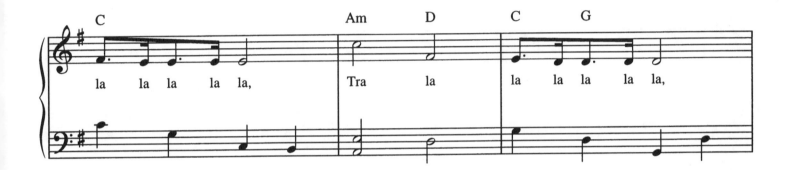

la la la la la, Tra la la la la la la,

Tra la la la la la la, Tra la la la la la la.

Verse 3:
Who'll toll the bell?
I, said the bull,
Because I can pull,
I'll toll the bell.

All the birds *etc.*

Verse 4:
Who'll dig his grave?
I, said the owl,
With my little trowel,
I'll dig his grave.

All the birds *etc.*

Verse 5:
Who'll be the parson?
I, said the rook,
With my bell and book,
I'll be the parson.

All the birds *etc.*

Verse 6:
Who'll be chief mourner?
I, said the dove,
I'll morn for my love,
I'll be chief mourner.

All the birds *etc.*

Where Is Thumbkin?

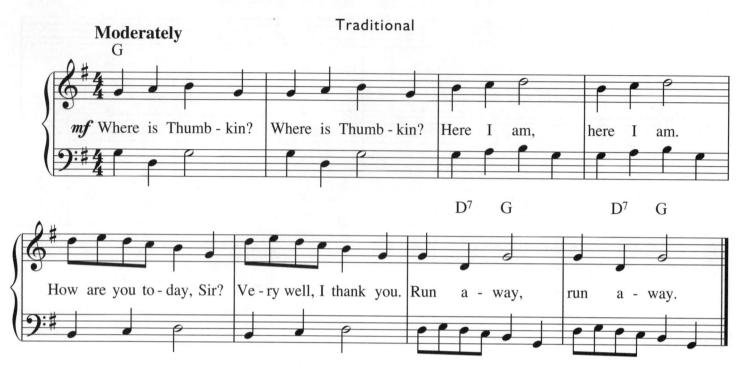

Verse 2:
Where is Pointer? *etc.*

Verse 3:
Where is Middle-man? *etc.*

Verse 4:
Where is Ring-man? *etc.*

Verse 5:
Where is Little-man? *etc.*

Why Doesn't My Goose?

Traditional

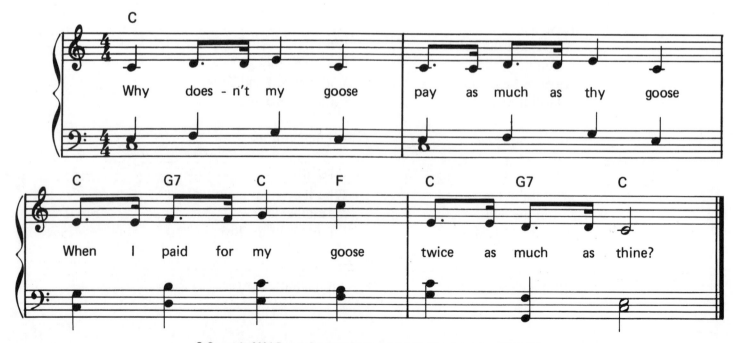

Yankee Doodle

Traditional

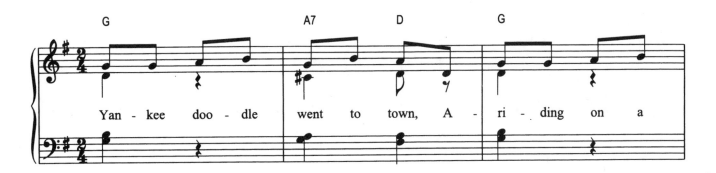

You'll Never Get To Heaven

Traditional

Chorus:
I ain't a-gonna grieve my Lord.
I ain't a-gonna grieve my Lord.
I ain't a-gonna grieve my Lord no more, no more.
I ain't a-gonna grieve my Lord.
I ain't a-gonna grieve my Lord.
I ain't a-gonna grieve my Lord no more.

Verse 2:
Oh you'll never get to heaven (oh you'll never
  get to heaven)
In a rocket ship (in a rocket ship)
'Cos a rocket ship ('cos a rocket ship)
Won't make the trip (won't make the trip)
Oh you'll never get to heaven in a rocket ship
'Cos a rocket ship won't make the trip,
I ain't a-gonna grieve my Lord no more.

I ain't a-gonna grieve my Lord. *etc.*

Verse 3:
Oh you'll never get to heaven (Oh you'll never
  get to heaven)
On an old tram car (On an old tram car)
'Cos an old tram car ('Cos an old tram car)
Won't get that far (Won't get that far)
Oh you'll never get to heaven on an old tram car
'Cos an old tram car won't get that far,
I ain't a-gonna grieve my Lord no more.

I ain't a-gonna grieve my Lord. *etc.*

Verse 4:
Oh you'll never get to heaven (oh you'll never
  get to heaven)
With Superman (with Superman)
'Cos the Lord he is ('cos the Lord he is)
A Batman fan (a Batman fan)
Oh you'll never get to heaven with Superman
'Cos the Lord he is a Batman fan,
I ain't a-gonna grieve my Lord no more.

I ain't a-gonna grieve my Lord. *etc.*

Verse 5:
Oh you'll never get to heaven (oh you'll never
  get to heaven)
In a Limousine (in a Limousine)
'Cos the Lord don't sell ('cos the Lord don't sell)
No gasoline (no gasoline)
Oh you'll never get to heaven in a Limousine
'Cos the Lord don't sell no gasoline,
I ain't a-gonna grieve my Lord no more.

I ain't a-gonna grieve my Lord. *etc.*

Printed in Malta by Progress Press Co. Ltd. 1/07 (61065)

Published by:
Chester Music Limited
8/9 Frith Street, London, W1D 3JB, England.

Exclusive Distributors:
Music Sales Limited
Distribution Centre, Newmarket Road, Bury St Edmunds, Suffolk, IP33 3YB, England.
Music Sales Corporation
257 Park Avenue South, New York, NY10010, United States of America.
Music Sales Pty Limited
120 Rothschild Avenue, Rosebery, NSW 2018, Australia.

Order No. CH68585
ISBN 1-84449-575-2
This book © Copyright 2004 by Chester Music.

Compiled by Heather Ramage.
Music processed by Note-orious Music Productions.
Designed & art directed by Michael Bell Design.
Illustrated by Rob Hefferan.